# Workbook

## *For*

# The Survival Guide for Kids with Behavior Challenges

How to Make Good Choices and Stay Out of

Trouble (Survival Guides for Kids)

**An Implementation Guide to Thomas McIntyre Book**

By

*Alex Sage publishing*

# Table of Contents

## How to use the workbook

# Introduction:

In today's fast-paced work environment, efficient organization and streamlined processes are paramount. One tool that can significantly enhance your productivity is a companion workbook, designed to complement and augment your primary work documents. This guide will walk you through the effective utilization of a "workbook page" within your companion workbook, offering practical insights to optimize your workflow.

## 1. Understanding the Companion Workbook:

Before delving into the specifics of a workbook page, it's crucial to grasp the concept of a companion workbook. This supplementary document is designed to support your primary work files, providing additional space for notes, calculations, or annotations. A workbook page is a dedicated section within this companion workbook, serving as a focal point for targeted tasks or information.

## 2. Identifying the Purpose:

Begin by clearly defining the purpose of the workbook page. Whether it's for brainstorming ideas, tracking progress, or annotating key information, a well-defined purpose will guide your use of the page and ensure that it aligns with your overall objectives.

### 3. Organizing Information:

Effectively organize the content on your workbook page to enhance clarity and accessibility. Utilize headers, bullet points, and other formatting options to create a visually appealing and easy-to-follow layout. This organization will not only facilitate your understanding but also make it convenient for others who may refer to the companion workbook.

### 4. Incorporating Visual Elements:

Enhance the workbook page by incorporating visual elements such as charts, graphs, or illustrations. Visual aids can convey complex information more efficiently and make the content more engaging. Ensure that these elements complement the textual information and contribute to a comprehensive understanding of the topic.

### 5. Utilizing Formulas and Functions:

If your workbook page involves numerical data or calculations, leverage the spreadsheet functionalities available. Incorporate formulas and functions to automate calculations, saving time and reducing the likelihood of errors. This feature is especially beneficial for tasks involving financial analysis, data tracking, or project management.

## 6. Maintaining Consistency:

Establish a consistent approach to using workbook pages throughout your companion workbook. This consistency promotes a standardized format, making it easier for you and your team to navigate and extract relevant information efficiently.

## 7. Regular Updates and Revisions:

Periodically revisit and update the content on your workbook pages to ensure relevance and accuracy. As your work progresses, new insights emerge, or circumstances change, keeping the companion workbook current will enhance its value as a dynamic reference tool.

## Conclusion:

Incorporating workbook pages into your companion workbook is a strategic approach to elevating your work processes. By understanding their purpose, organizing information effectively, and leveraging visual elements and functions, you can maximize the utility of these pages. Consistency and regular updates are key to ensuring that your companion workbook remains a valuable asset in your professional toolkit, supporting your success in the dynamic world of work.

## Summary of the book

### Introduction:

"The Survival Guide for Kids with Behavior Challenges: How to Make Good Choices and Stay out of Trouble" by Thomas McIntyre is an invaluable resource designed to empower children facing behavior challenges with the knowledge and skills needed to navigate life successfully. As part of the "Survival Guides for Kids" series, McIntyre combines his expertise as a psychologist and educator to create a comprehensive guide that fosters personal growth, self-awareness, and positive decision-making.

### Overview:

The book begins by addressing the importance of self-awareness, encouraging readers to understand their own behavior and its impact on themselves and those around them. McIntyre employs a compassionate and non-judgmental tone, creating a safe space for children to explore and reflect on their actions. The guide then delves into practical strategies, offering step-by-step advice on making positive choices and developing effective problem-solving skills.

### Key Themes:

### 1. Understanding Behavior Challenges:

McIntyre starts by elucidating the nature of behavior challenges, helping children recognize and accept their unique struggles. By fostering self-compassion, the author lays the groundwork for constructive change.

## 2. Self-Reflection and Awareness:

The guide encourages readers to reflect on their actions, thoughts, and emotions. Through various exercises and examples, McIntyre provides tools for increased self-awareness, allowing children to identify triggers and patterns in their behavior.

## 3. Building Empathy:

One of the notable aspects of the book is its emphasis on empathy. McIntyre illustrates the importance of understanding others' perspectives and feelings, fostering compassion as a foundation for improved social interactions.

## 4. Effective Communication:

The author emphasizes the significance of clear and assertive communication. Practical tips and scenarios are provided to help children express themselves effectively, reducing misunderstandings and conflicts.

## 5. Decision-Making Skills:

McIntyre provides a structured approach to decision-making, helping children evaluate choices, consider consequences, and make informed decisions. This empowers them to take control of their actions and move towards positive outcomes.

## 6. Problem-Solving Techniques:

The guide introduces various problem-solving techniques, equipping children with the tools to navigate challenges and conflicts. McIntyre emphasizes resilience and perseverance as key components of successful problem-solving.

**7. Practical Tips for Daily Life:**

Real-life scenarios and relatable examples are woven throughout the book, making the content accessible and applicable to everyday situations. McIntyre provides practical tips that children can easily implement to overcome challenges and make better choices.

**Conclusion:**

"The Survival Guide for Kids with Behavior Challenges" by Thomas McIntyre stands as a beacon of support for children facing behavior challenges. Through a combination of expert insights, relatable examples, and practical strategies, McIntyre empowers young readers to make positive choices, fostering personal growth and resilience. This invaluable resource serves as a guiding light, promoting self-discovery and laying the foundation for a brighter, more successful future.

# What's Your Starting Point?
## Key Lessons

1. Self-awareness is Crucial: The book emphasizes the importance of understanding oneself, and acknowledging personal strengths, weaknesses, and triggers for behavior challenges.
2. Choices Determine Outcomes: It highlights the power of choices and how they impact the course of one's life. By making conscious decisions, kids can shape positive outcomes for themselves.
3. Building Resilience: The book underscores the value of resilience in facing challenges. It provides strategies for bouncing back from setbacks and learning from difficult situations.
4. Empathy and Understanding: Kids are encouraged to develop empathy and understanding towards others, recognizing that everyone has their starting point and struggles.
5. Goal Setting and Planning: Setting goals and creating a plan to achieve them is a key aspect of navigating behavior challenges. The book guides kids in developing realistic and achievable goals.

## Reflection Questions

1. What are some of your strengths that can be harnessed to overcome behavior challenges?

-----------------------------------------------------------------

-----------------------------------------------------------------

------------------------------------------------

------------------------------------------------

------------------------------------------------

------------------------------------------------

2. In challenging situations, how do you typically react, and what strategies can you employ to make better choices?

------------------------------------------------

------------------------------------------------

------------------------------------------------

------------------------------------------------

------------------------------------------------

------------------------------------------------

3. What choices have you made recently that contributed to positive outcomes in your life?

------------------------------------------------

------------------------------------------------

------------------------------------------------

------------------------------------------------

------------------------------------------------

------------------------------------------------

4. How do you handle setbacks, and what can you do to build greater resilience in challenging times?

------------------------------------------------

------------------------------------------------

------------------------------------------------

------------------------------------------------

------------------------------------------------

------------------------------------------------

5. Consider your interactions with others. How can you show more empathy and understanding toward their starting points and struggles?

------------------------------------------------

------------------------------------------------

------------------------------------------------

------------------------------------------------

------------------------------------------------

------------------------------------------------

6. What goals have you set for yourself in terms of behavior improvement, and what steps can you take to achieve them?

----------------------------------------------------------------

----------------------------------------------------------------

----------------------------------------------------------------

----------------------------------------------------------------

----------------------------------------------------------------

----------------------------------------------------------------

7. Reflect on a recent situation where you faced a behavior challenge. How could a different choice have led to a more positive outcome?

----------------------------------------------------------------

----------------------------------------------------------------

----------------------------------------------------------------

----------------------------------------------------------------

----------------------------------------------------------------

----------------------------------------------------------------

8. Think about someone you admire for their

behavior and choices. What qualities do they possess that you can incorporate into your own life?

------------------------------------------------

------------------------------------------------

------------------------------------------------

------------------------------------------------

------------------------------------------------

------------------------------------------------

9. Consider your support system. How can you communicate your goals and challenges to those around you for additional support?

------------------------------------------------

------------------------------------------------

------------------------------------------------

------------------------------------------------

------------------------------------------------

------------------------------------------------

10. In planning for the future, what steps can you

take to create a positive starting point for yourself in various aspects of your life?

-------------------------------------------------------------
-------------------------------------------------------------
-------------------------------------------------------------
-------------------------------------------------------------
-------------------------------------------------------------
-------------------------------------------------------------

## Four Smart Choice for Dealing with Feelings:

## How can I tell the difference between a bad choice and a smart one?

### Key Lessons

1. Understanding Consequences: The book emphasizes the importance of considering the potential consequences of your choices, helping you differentiate between actions that lead to positive outcomes and those that may result in trouble.

2. Emotional Awareness: Learn to identify and manage your emotions. The book teaches you how to recognize emotional triggers and make choices

based on rational thinking rather than impulsive reactions.

3. Developing Empathy: Gain insights into the feelings and perspectives of others. This skill is crucial for making choices that not only benefit you but also consider the well-being of those around you.

4. Building Self-Regulation: Develop self-control and discipline to resist making impulsive or harmful decisions. The book provides strategies for staying calm under pressure and making thoughtful choices even in challenging situations.

5. Effective Communication: Learn the importance of clear and respectful communication. This skill helps in navigating conflicts and making choices that promote positive relationships with others.

## Reflection Questions

1. How can you apply the concept of considering consequences to your decision-making process in daily life?

------------------------------------------------------------

------------------------------------------------------------

------------------------------------------------------------

------------------------------------------------------------

------------------------------------------------------------

------------------------------------------------------------

2. In what ways can you become more aware of your emotions and use that awareness to make smarter choices?

------------------------------------------------

------------------------------------------------

------------------------------------------------

------------------------------------------------

------------------------------------------------

------------------------------------------------

3. Reflect on a situation where understanding someone else's perspective could have led to a better choice. How will you incorporate empathy into future decisions?

------------------------------------------------

------------------------------------------------

------------------------------------------------

------------------------------------------------

------------------------------------------------

------------------------------------------------

4. Share a personal experience where impulsive behavior led to negative consequences. What strategies can you employ to enhance self-regulation and prevent similar situations?

-----------------------------------------------------------

-----------------------------------------------------------

-----------------------------------------------------------

-----------------------------------------------------------

-----------------------------------------------------------

-----------------------------------------------------------

5. Consider a recent decision where effective communication played a crucial role. How can you improve your communication skills to make better choices in the future?

-----------------------------------------------------------

-----------------------------------------------------------

-----------------------------------------------------------

-----------------------------------------------------------

-----------------------------------------------------------

---------------------------------------------------------------

6. How do you currently evaluate the potential impact of your choices on your relationships with friends and family? What steps can you take to strengthen these connections through your decisions?

---------------------------------------------------------------

---------------------------------------------------------------

---------------------------------------------------------------

---------------------------------------------------------------

---------------------------------------------------------------

---------------------------------------------------------------

7. Reflect on a time when you successfully navigated a challenging situation. What skills did you utilize, and how can you apply them to upcoming decisions?

---------------------------------------------------------------

---------------------------------------------------------------

---------------------------------------------------------------

---------------------------------------------------------------

---------------------------------------------------------------

---------------------------------------------------------------

8. Analyze a recent choice that aligned with your values and principles. How can you consistently make decisions that reflect your core beliefs?

---------------------------------------------------------------

---------------------------------------------------------------

---------------------------------------------------------------

---------------------------------------------------------------

---------------------------------------------------------------

---------------------------------------------------------------

9. Identify a decision-making pattern that may not be serving your best interests. What changes can you implement to break this pattern and make smarter choices?

---------------------------------------------------------------

---------------------------------------------------------------

---------------------------------------------------------------

----------------------------------------------------

----------------------------------------------------

----------------------------------------------------

10. Consider the role of peer pressure in your decision-making. How can you build resilience and assertiveness to make choices that align with your values, even in the face of external influences?

----------------------------------------------------

----------------------------------------------------

----------------------------------------------------

----------------------------------------------------

----------------------------------------------------

----------------------------------------------------

## Build your self-esteem:

## Key Lessons

1. Recognize Your Strengths: Take time to identify your unique qualities and abilities. Acknowledge and appreciate the things you excel at, whether they are academic, creative, or social.

2. Embrace Imperfections: Understand that everyone makes mistakes, and that doesn't diminish your worth. Embrace imperfections as opportunities to learn and grow, rather than as reasons to feel inadequate.

3. Set Realistic Goals: Break down your larger objectives into smaller, achievable goals. Celebrate your successes along the way, and use setbacks as opportunities to reassess and adjust your plans.

4. Practice Self-Compassion: Treat yourself with kindness and understanding, especially during challenging times. Develop a positive inner dialogue that encourages self-compassion rather than self-criticism.

5. Surround Yourself with Positive Influences: Seek out relationships and environments that uplift and support you. Surrounding yourself with positivity can contribute significantly to building and maintaining self-esteem.

## Reflection Questions

1. What are some of your unique strengths and talents that you can appreciate and build upon?

------------------------------------------------------------

------------------------------------------------------------

------------------------------------------------------------

------------------------------------------------------------

-------------------------------------------------------

-------------------------------------------------------

2. How do you react when you make a mistake, and how can you shift your perspective to see it as an opportunity for growth?

-------------------------------------------------------

-------------------------------------------------------

-------------------------------------------------------

-------------------------------------------------------

-------------------------------------------------------

-------------------------------------------------------

3. What are some small, achievable goals you can set for yourself to boost your confidence and self-esteem?

-------------------------------------------------------

-------------------------------------------------------

-------------------------------------------------------

-------------------------------------------------------

-------------------------------------------------------

----------------------------------------------------------------

4. How can you be more compassionate towards yourself, especially in challenging situations?

----------------------------------------------------------------

----------------------------------------------------------------

----------------------------------------------------------------

----------------------------------------------------------------

----------------------------------------------------------------

----------------------------------------------------------------

5. In what ways can you celebrate your successes, no matter how small, to reinforce a positive self-image?

----------------------------------------------------------------

----------------------------------------------------------------

----------------------------------------------------------------

----------------------------------------------------------------

----------------------------------------------------------------

----------------------------------------------------------------

6. Who are the people in your life that contribute

positively to your self-esteem, and how can you nurture those relationships?

------------------------------------------------------------

------------------------------------------------------------

------------------------------------------------------------

------------------------------------------------------------

------------------------------------------------------------

------------------------------------------------------------

7. What are some self-compassionate phrases you can use to encourage yourself during tough times?

------------------------------------------------------------

------------------------------------------------------------

------------------------------------------------------------

------------------------------------------------------------

------------------------------------------------------------

------------------------------------------------------------

8. How can you create a supportive environment for yourself, both at home and at school?

-----------------------------------------------

-----------------------------------------------

-----------------------------------------------

-----------------------------------------------

-----------------------------------------------

-----------------------------------------------

9. Are there any negative influences in your life that may be affecting your self-esteem, and how can you minimize their impact?

-----------------------------------------------

-----------------------------------------------

-----------------------------------------------

-----------------------------------------------

-----------------------------------------------

-----------------------------------------------

10. What steps can you take to surround yourself with more positivity and encouragement daily?

-----------------------------------------------

-----------------------------------------------

----------------------------------------------------------

----------------------------------------------------------

----------------------------------------------------------

----------------------------------------------------------

## Talk with someone you trust:
## Key Lessons

1. Open Communication is Vital: Talking with someone you trust fosters open communication, allowing for the expression of thoughts and feelings without judgment.
2. Gain Different Perspectives: Conversations with a trusted individual can provide valuable insights and alternative perspectives, helping you see situations from different angles.
3. Emotional Support Matters: Sharing your thoughts and concerns with someone you trust can provide emotional support, making it easier to navigate challenging situations.
4. Problem-Solving Together: Engaging in conversations allows you to work together with someone you trust to find solutions to problems or challenges you may be facing.
5. Builds Stronger Relationships: Regular communication with a trusted person strengthens the bond between you, creating a supportive network that enhances your overall well-being.

## Reflection Questions

1. How do you feel when you talk with someone you trust about your challenges or concerns?

------------------------------------------------

------------------------------------------------

------------------------------------------------

------------------------------------------------

------------------------------------------------

------------------------------------------------

2. Can you recall a specific instance where discussing a problem with someone you trust helped you gain a new perspective?

------------------------------------------------

------------------------------------------------

------------------------------------------------

------------------------------------------------

------------------------------------------------

------------------------------------------------

3. How does having a conversation with a trusted

individual contribute to your emotional well-being?

_____

_____

_____

_____

_____

_____

4. In what ways has talking with someone you trust helped you solve problems more effectively than trying to handle them on your own?

_____

_____

_____

_____

_____

_____

5. How do you think open communication with a

trusted person strengthens your relationship with them?

---------------------------------------------------

---------------------------------------------------

---------------------------------------------------

---------------------------------------------------

---------------------------------------------------

---------------------------------------------------

6. What strategies can you use to ensure that your conversations with someone you trust remain respectful and non-judgmental?

---------------------------------------------------

---------------------------------------------------

---------------------------------------------------

---------------------------------------------------

---------------------------------------------------

---------------------------------------------------

7. How do you typically approach seeking advice

or support from someone you trust? Are there specific challenges you face in doing so?

-----------------------------------------------------------

-----------------------------------------------------------

-----------------------------------------------------------

-----------------------------------------------------------

-----------------------------------------------------------

-----------------------------------------------------------

8. Reflect on a time when a conversation with a trusted individual helped you navigate a difficult decision. What did you learn from that experience?

-----------------------------------------------------------

-----------------------------------------------------------

-----------------------------------------------------------

-----------------------------------------------------------

-----------------------------------------------------------

-----------------------------------------------------------

9. How can the habit of talking with someone you

trust be incorporated into your routine to enhance your overall well-being?

-----------------------------------------------------------

-----------------------------------------------------------

-----------------------------------------------------------

-----------------------------------------------------------

-----------------------------------------------------------

-----------------------------------------------------------

10. Consider the impact of regularly communicating with a trusted person on your ability to cope with stress and make positive choices. What changes can you make to strengthen this aspect of your life?

-----------------------------------------------------------

-----------------------------------------------------------

-----------------------------------------------------------

-----------------------------------------------------------

-----------------------------------------------------------

---

## Write or draw:

## Key Lessons

1. Expression through Writing or Drawing:
   - Learn the importance of expressing yourself through writing or drawing as a healthy outlet for emotions.
2. Self-Reflection:
   - Understand the power of self-reflection through creative activities to gain insights into your thoughts and behaviors.
3. Problem-Solving Skills:
   - Develop problem-solving skills by using writing or drawing to explore alternative solutions to challenges you may be facing.
4. Emotional Regulation:
   - Use writing or drawing as a tool to regulate and manage your emotions, helping you make better choices in various situations.
5. Communication Skills:
   - Improve communication skills by expressing thoughts and feelings through written or visual means, fostering better understanding with others.

## Reflection Questions

1. How can you incorporate writing or drawing into your daily routine to help process your emotions?

---------------------------------------------------------

---------------------------------------------------------

---------------------------------------------------------

---------------------------------------------------------

---------------------------------------------------------

---------------------------------------------------------

2. In what ways do you believe self-reflection through creative activities can positively impact your decision-making?

---------------------------------------------------------

---------------------------------------------------------

---------------------------------------------------------

---------------------------------------------------------

---------------------------------------------------------

---------------------------------------------------------

3. What are some challenges you've faced recently, and how might you use writing or drawing to explore potential solutions?

-------------------------------------------------

-------------------------------------------------

-------------------------------------------------

-------------------------------------------------

-------------------------------------------------

-------------------------------------------------

4. How do you currently manage your emotions, and how can incorporating creative expression enhance your emotional regulation?

-------------------------------------------------

-------------------------------------------------

-------------------------------------------------

-------------------------------------------------

-------------------------------------------------

-------------------------------------------------

5. Consider a recent communication breakdown. How might expressing your thoughts through writing or drawing have improved the situation?

----------------------------------------

----------------------------------------

----------------------------------------

----------------------------------------

----------------------------------------

----------------------------------------

6. What topics or themes do you find most compelling to write or draw about, and why?

----------------------------------------

----------------------------------------

----------------------------------------

----------------------------------------

----------------------------------------

----------------------------------------

7. How can creative expression serve as a tool for self-discovery and personal growth in your life?

----------------------------------------

----------------------------------------

----------------------------------------

----------------------------------------

------------------------------------------------------------

------------------------------------------------------------

8. Think about a recent conflict. How might documenting your perspective through writing or drawing help others understand your point of view?

------------------------------------------------------------

------------------------------------------------------------

------------------------------------------------------------

------------------------------------------------------------

------------------------------------------------------------

------------------------------------------------------------

9. In what ways can you use writing or drawing as a positive coping mechanism during challenging times?

------------------------------------------------------------

------------------------------------------------------------

------------------------------------------------------------

------------------------------------------------------------

-----------------------------------------------------------

-----------------------------------------------------------

10. Reflect on past success. How might capturing that moment through words or images inspire and motivate you in the future?

-----------------------------------------------------------

-----------------------------------------------------------

-----------------------------------------------------------

-----------------------------------------------------------

-----------------------------------------------------------

-----------------------------------------------------------

## Chill out or get moving:
## Key Lessons

1. Understanding Your Emotions:
In this chapter, you'll learn the importance of recognizing and understanding your emotions. Whether its stress, anger, or excitement, being aware of your feelings is the first step towards making positive choices.
2. The Power of Taking a Pause:

Discover the value of taking a moment to pause and reflect before reacting impulsively. The chapter emphasizes how a brief break can help you regain control over your emotions and make better decisions.

3. Exploring Calming Strategies:
Explore various calming strategies that suit your personality and situation. From deep breathing exercises to finding a quiet space, this chapter provides practical tips for managing stress and anxiety effectively.

4. Importance of Physical Activity:
Recognize the connection between physical activity and emotional well-being. Whether it's going for a walk, playing a sport, or engaging in any form of exercise, staying active can significantly impact your mood and decision-making.

5. Developing a Personal Coping Plan:
Learn how to create a personalized coping plan to navigate challenging situations. By combining the strategies discussed in the chapter, you'll be equipped with a toolkit to handle behavior challenges more effectively.

## Reflection Questions

1. How do you typically recognize and label your emotions in challenging situations?

----------------------------------------

----------------------------------------

----------------------------------------

----------------------------------------

----------------------------------------

----------------------------------------

2. In what ways can taking a brief pause benefit you when facing behavior challenges?

----------------------------------------

----------------------------------------

----------------------------------------

----------------------------------------

----------------------------------------

----------------------------------------

3. What specific calming strategies resonate with you, and how can you incorporate them into your daily routine?

----------------------------------------

----------------------------------------

------------------------------------------------

------------------------------------------------

------------------------------------------------

------------------------------------------------

4. Have you experienced a positive change in your emotions after engaging in physical activity? How can you integrate more movement into your routine?

------------------------------------------------

------------------------------------------------

------------------------------------------------

------------------------------------------------

------------------------------------------------

------------------------------------------------

5. What are some proactive steps you can take to prevent behavior challenges, based on the lessons learned in this chapter?

------------------------------------------------

------------------------------------------------

---------------------------------------------------------------

---------------------------------------------------------------

---------------------------------------------------------------

---------------------------------------------------------------

6. How can you create a personalized coping plan that aligns with your unique preferences and needs?

---------------------------------------------------------------

---------------------------------------------------------------

---------------------------------------------------------------

---------------------------------------------------------------

---------------------------------------------------------------

---------------------------------------------------------------

7. Are there any specific situations or triggers where you find it particularly challenging to chill out or get moving? How can you address these challenges?

---------------------------------------------------------------

---------------------------------------------------------------

------------------------------------------------

------------------------------------------------

------------------------------------------------

------------------------------------------------

8. What support systems or resources can you tap into when you need assistance in implementing the strategies discussed in the chapter?

------------------------------------------------

------------------------------------------------

------------------------------------------------

------------------------------------------------

------------------------------------------------

------------------------------------------------

9. How do you currently handle stress, and are there alternative methods mentioned in the chapter that you would like to try?

------------------------------------------------

------------------------------------------------

------------------------------------------------

----------------------------------------------------------------

----------------------------------------------------------------

----------------------------------------------------------------

10. What long-term goals can you set for yourself in terms of incorporating these lessons into your daily life? How will you measure your progress over time?

----------------------------------------------------------------

----------------------------------------------------------------

----------------------------------------------------------------

----------------------------------------------------------------

----------------------------------------------------------------

----------------------------------------------------------------

## Another Smart Choice for Dealing with Feelings:
## Stop, think, choose, and think again:
## Key Lessons

1. Pause and Reflect: Taking a moment to stop and think before making a decision allows you to consider the consequences and alternatives.

2. Empowerment through Choice: Recognize that you have the power to make choices that align with your values and goals.

3. Decision-Making Skills: Develop the skill of thoughtful decision-making by weighing the pros and cons before taking action.

4. Learn from Mistakes: Understand that making mistakes is a part of life, but reflecting on them provides an opportunity for growth.

5. Consistency in Choices: Cultivate a habit of consistently making positive choices to build a foundation for a successful and fulfilling life.

## Reflection Questions

1. How do you feel about the idea of taking a moment to stop and think before making decisions?

------------------------------------------------------------

------------------------------------------------------------

------------------------------------------------------------

------------------------------------------------------------

------------------------------------------------------------

------------------------------------------------------------

2. In what ways do you believe empowering yourself through choice can positively impact your life?

--------------------------------------------------------

--------------------------------------------------------

--------------------------------------------------------

--------------------------------------------------------

--------------------------------------------------------

--------------------------------------------------------

3. Can you recall a situation where your decision-making skills played a crucial role in the outcome?

--------------------------------------------------------

--------------------------------------------------------

--------------------------------------------------------

--------------------------------------------------------

--------------------------------------------------------

--------------------------------------------------------

4. How do you typically handle mistakes, and what have you learned from them in the past?

------------------------------------------

------------------------------------------

------------------------------------------

------------------------------------------

------------------------------------------

------------------------------------------

5. Reflect on the power of consistency in making positive choices. How can this practice contribute to your long-term well-being?

------------------------------------------

------------------------------------------

------------------------------------------

------------------------------------------

------------------------------------------

------------------------------------------

6. What strategies can you implement to remind yourself to "stop, think, choose, and think again" in various situations?

---------------------------------------------------------------

---------------------------------------------------------------

---------------------------------------------------------------

---------------------------------------------------------------

---------------------------------------------------------------

---------------------------------------------------------------

7. How might the concept of thoughtful decision-making apply to both small, everyday choices and larger, more significant decisions?

---------------------------------------------------------------

---------------------------------------------------------------

---------------------------------------------------------------

---------------------------------------------------------------

---------------------------------------------------------------

---------------------------------------------------------------

8. Consider the role of peer influence in your decision-making process. How can you stay true to your values when faced with external pressures?

------------------------------------------------------------

------------------------------------------------------------

------------------------------------------------------------

------------------------------------------------------------

------------------------------------------------------------

------------------------------------------------------------

9. Reflect on the relationship between self-discipline and making good choices. How can you strengthen your self-discipline in decision-making?

------------------------------------------------------------

------------------------------------------------------------

------------------------------------------------------------

------------------------------------------------------------

------------------------------------------------------------

------------------------------------------------------------

10. In what areas of your life do you see the most significant potential for positive change through implementing the "stop, think, choose, and think again" approach?

--------------------------------------------------------

--------------------------------------------------------

--------------------------------------------------------

--------------------------------------------------------

--------------------------------------------------------

--------------------------------------------------------

## Three Survival skills for Dealing with difficult people:

### Ignore mean words and actions:
### Key Lessons

1. Understanding Others: Recognize that people may have their challenges and difficulties, which can sometimes lead to mean words and actions. Empathize with their struggles rather than taking their behavior personally.

2. Power of Ignoring: Learn the strength in choosing not to react to mean words or actions. Ignoring negative behavior can help diffuse situations and prevent escalation, giving you greater control over your responses.

3. Building Resilience: Develop resilience by understanding that means words and actions do not define your worth. Focus on your strengths and

positive qualities, rather than letting negativity affect your self-esteem.

4. Seeking Support: Identify trustworthy individuals, such as friends, family, or teachers, who can offer guidance and support when faced with mean words or actions. Share your experiences and feelings with those who genuinely care about your well-being.

5. Choosing Battles Wisely: Learn to discern between situations that require a response and those that are best ignored. Not every mean comment or action warrants a reaction; sometimes, it's more empowering to let things go.

## Reflection Questions

1. How do you typically feel when someone directs mean words or actions toward you, and how might ignoring them positively impact your emotions?

------------------------------------------------------------

------------------------------------------------------------

------------------------------------------------------------

------------------------------------------------------------

------------------------------------------------------------

------------------------------------------------------------

2. In what situations do you find it most challenging to ignore mean behavior, and how can you prepare yourself to stay composed in those moments?

---------------------------------------------------------------

---------------------------------------------------------------

---------------------------------------------------------------

---------------------------------------------------------------

---------------------------------------------------------------

---------------------------------------------------------------

3. Reflect on a time when you successfully ignored mean words or actions. What strategies did you employ, and what positive outcomes resulted from your choice?

---------------------------------------------------------------

---------------------------------------------------------------

---------------------------------------------------------------

---------------------------------------------------------------

---------------------------------------------------------------

--------------------------------------------------------------

4. Consider the idea that people who behave negatively may be facing their difficulties. How can understanding their perspective help you in ignoring their mean words or actions?

--------------------------------------------------------------

--------------------------------------------------------------

--------------------------------------------------------------

--------------------------------------------------------------

--------------------------------------------------------------

--------------------------------------------------------------

5. How does the power of ignoring contribute to a sense of control in challenging situations, and how can this sense of control positively impact your overall well-being?

--------------------------------------------------------------

--------------------------------------------------------------

--------------------------------------------------------------

--------------------------------------------------------------

-------------------------------------------------------------

-------------------------------------------------------------

6. Reflect on the role of resilience in ignoring mean behavior. How can focusing on your strengths and positive qualities help you navigate challenging social situations?

-------------------------------------------------------------

-------------------------------------------------------------

-------------------------------------------------------------

-------------------------------------------------------------

-------------------------------------------------------------

-------------------------------------------------------------

7. Identify individuals in your life whom you trust and can turn to for support when faced with mean words or actions. How can you strengthen these support networks?

-------------------------------------------------------------

-------------------------------------------------------------

-------------------------------------------------------------

---------------------------------------------------------

---------------------------------------------------------

---------------------------------------------------------

8. Consider the concept of choosing battles wisely. In what instances is it more beneficial for you to ignore negativity, and when might it be necessary to address the behavior?

---------------------------------------------------------

---------------------------------------------------------

---------------------------------------------------------

---------------------------------------------------------

---------------------------------------------------------

---------------------------------------------------------

9. How can the skill of ignoring mean words and actions contribute to your personal growth and development, both socially and emotionally?

---------------------------------------------------------

---------------------------------------------------------

---------------------------------------------------------

---------------------------------------------------------------

---------------------------------------------------------------

---------------------------------------------------------------

10. Reflect on the long-term impact of consistently choosing to ignore negativity. How might this skill positively shape your relationships and interactions over time?

---------------------------------------------------------------

---------------------------------------------------------------

---------------------------------------------------------------

---------------------------------------------------------------

---------------------------------------------------------------

---------------------------------------------------------------

## Be assertive:

### Key Lessons

1. Understanding Assertiveness:
   - Learn what it means to be assertive and how it differs from being passive or aggressive.
2. Expressing Feelings:
   - Discover the importance of expressing your feelings and needs clearly and respectfully.

3. Setting Boundaries:
  - Develop the skill of setting healthy boundaries to protect yourself and maintain positive relationships.
4. Saying "No" with Confidence:
  - Gain the confidence to say "no" when necessary, while still being respectful and considerate of others.
5. Problem-Solving Strategies:
  - Acquire problem-solving strategies to handle conflicts and challenges assertively and constructively.

## Reflection Questions

1. Understanding Assertiveness:
  - How do you define assertiveness, and why is it important in your interactions with others?

-------------------------------------------------------------

-------------------------------------------------------------

-------------------------------------------------------------

-------------------------------------------------------------

-------------------------------------------------------------

-------------------------------------------------------------

2. Expressing Feelings:

  - Can you think of a recent situation where expressing your feelings would have been beneficial, and how could you have done it assertively?

---------------------------------------------------------

---------------------------------------------------------

---------------------------------------------------------

---------------------------------------------------------

---------------------------------------------------------

---------------------------------------------------------

3. Setting Boundaries:

 - Reflect on your current boundaries with friends and family. Are there areas where you need to establish clearer boundaries to protect yourself?

---------------------------------------------------------

---------------------------------------------------------

---------------------------------------------------------

---------------------------------------------------------

---------------------------------------------------------

---------------------------------------------------------

4. Saying "No" with Confidence:

- Think about a recent request you found difficult to decline. How could you have said "no" assertively while still being considerate?

------------------------------------------------

------------------------------------------------

------------------------------------------------

------------------------------------------------

------------------------------------------------

------------------------------------------------

5. Problem-Solving Strategies:

- Consider a recent conflict you faced. How did you handle it, and what assertive problem-solving strategies could you apply in similar situations?

------------------------------------------------

------------------------------------------------

------------------------------------------------

------------------------------------------------

------------------------------------------------

------------------------------------------------

6. Recognizing Passive Behavior:

- In what situations do you tend to display passive behavior, and how might being more assertive benefit you in those instances?

------------------------------------------------------------

------------------------------------------------------------

------------------------------------------------------------

------------------------------------------------------------

------------------------------------------------------------

------------------------------------------------------------

## 7. Identifying Aggressive Behavior:

- Reflect on times when you may have been aggressive. How can you modify your approach to express your needs assertively rather than aggressively?

------------------------------------------------------------

------------------------------------------------------------

------------------------------------------------------------

------------------------------------------------------------

------------------------------------------------------------

## 8. Building Self-Confidence:

- Identify one area where you'd like to boost your self-confidence. How can being more assertive contribute to building that confidence?

---------------------------------------------------------------

---------------------------------------------------------------

---------------------------------------------------------------

---------------------------------------------------------------

---------------------------------------------------------------

---------------------------------------------------------------

9. Acknowledging Others' Perspectives:

- Consider a recent disagreement with someone. How could acknowledging the other person's perspective and expressing your own assertively improve the situation?

---------------------------------------------------------------

---------------------------------------------------------------

---------------------------------------------------------------

---------------------------------------------------------------

---------------------------------------------------------------

---------------------------------------------------------------

10. Setting Personal Goals:

- What are some personal goals you have for being more assertive in different aspects of your life, and how do you plan to work towards them?

---------------------------------------------------------------

---------------------------------------------------------------

---------------------------------------------------------------

---------------------------------------------------------------

---------------------------------------------------------------

---------------------------------------------------------------

## Say "I" instead of "You"
## Key Lessons

1. Personal Responsibility:
   - Learn to express feelings and thoughts using "I" statements to take ownership of your emotions and opinions.
2. Effective Communication:

   - Discover the power of clear communication by stating personal needs and experiences without blaming others.
3. Building Empathy:

   - Understand how using "I" statements can foster empathy and create a more constructive dialogue with others.
4. Conflict Resolution:

- Develop conflict resolution skills by articulating your perspective without placing blame, fostering a more collaborative problem-solving approach.

5. Self-awareness:

- Cultivate self-awareness by recognizing the impact of language choices on personal well-being and relationships.

## Reflection Questions

1. Communication Style:
- How often do you find yourself using "you" statements when expressing your feelings or opinions?

------------------------------------------------------------

------------------------------------------------------------

------------------------------------------------------------

------------------------------------------------------------

------------------------------------------------------------

------------------------------------------------------------

2. Ownership of Emotions:

- In what situations could using "I" statements improve the way you communicate your emotions and needs?

---------------------------------------------------------------

---------------------------------------------------------------

---------------------------------------------------------------

---------------------------------------------------------------

---------------------------------------------------------------

---------------------------------------------------------------

## 3. Impact on Others:

- Reflect on a recent interaction. How might using "I" statements have influenced the other person's perception and response?

---------------------------------------------------------------

---------------------------------------------------------------

---------------------------------------------------------------

---------------------------------------------------------------

---------------------------------------------------------------

---------------------------------------------------------------

## 4. Building Empathy:

- How can adopting the "I" statement approach enhance your ability to understand and empathize with others?

-------------------------------------------------

-------------------------------------------------

-------------------------------------------------

-------------------------------------------------

-------------------------------------------------

-------------------------------------------------

## 5. Conflict Resolution Strategies:

- Consider a recent disagreement. How might using "I" statements have changed the dynamics and outcomes of the conflict?

-------------------------------------------------

-------------------------------------------------

-------------------------------------------------

-------------------------------------------------

-------------------------------------------------

-------------------------------------------------

## 6. Accountability:

- When facing challenges, how can framing your experiences using "I" statements contribute to a sense of personal responsibility?

---------------------------------------------

---------------------------------------------

---------------------------------------------

---------------------------------------------

---------------------------------------------

---------------------------------------------

## 7. Effective Feedback:

- How might incorporating "I" statements enhance the way you provide feedback to others?

---------------------------------------------

---------------------------------------------

---------------------------------------------

---------------------------------------------

---------------------------------------------

---------------------------------------------

## 8. Language and Respect:

- Reflect on instances where using "you" statements may have unintentionally conveyed disrespect. How can shifting to "I" statements improve respect in communication?

------------------------------------------------

------------------------------------------------

------------------------------------------------

------------------------------------------------

------------------------------------------------

------------------------------------------------

## 9. Creating a Positive Environment:

- How can adopting the practice of saying "I" instead of "you" contribute to a more positive and open atmosphere in your relationships?

------------------------------------------------

------------------------------------------------

------------------------------------------------

------------------------------------------------

------------------------------------------------

------------------------------------------------

## 10. Continuous Improvement:

- What steps can you take to consistently use "I" statements and improve your communication skills over time?

-------------------------------------------------------

-------------------------------------------------------

-------------------------------------------------------

-------------------------------------------------------

-------------------------------------------------------

-------------------------------------------------------

## Ways to help yourself make good choices in school:
### Key Lessons

1. Anticipate Challenges: Being prepared involves recognizing potential challenges and developing strategies to overcome them.
2. Develop a Plan: Create a proactive plan for various situations, helping you respond thoughtfully instead of reacting impulsively.
3. Resourcefulness: Learn to utilize available resources effectively, enhancing your ability to navigate challenging circumstances.
4. Adaptability: Being prepared also means staying flexible and adapting your plans as needed in response to changing situations.
5. Self-Awareness: Understand your strengths and weaknesses to better prepare for challenges, enabling personal growth and resilience.

## Reflection Questions

1. How do you and your peers typically handle unexpected challenges?

------------------------------------------------

------------------------------------------------

------------------------------------------------

------------------------------------------------

------------------------------------------------

------------------------------------------------

2. In what ways have you and your friends successfully prepared for upcoming events or situations in the past?

------------------------------------------------

------------------------------------------------

------------------------------------------------

------------------------------------------------

------------------------------------------------

------------------------------------------------

3. Can you identify specific situations where being prepared would have made a significant difference

in the outcome? What would you do differently now?

---------------------------------------------------------------

---------------------------------------------------------------

---------------------------------------------------------------

---------------------------------------------------------------

---------------------------------------------------------------

---------------------------------------------------------------

4. How do you and your family or friends communicate and collaborate to ensure everyone is prepared for shared activities or events?

---------------------------------------------------------------

---------------------------------------------------------------

---------------------------------------------------------------

---------------------------------------------------------------

---------------------------------------------------------------

---------------------------------------------------------------

5. What resources, both internal and external, do

you and your peers have at your disposal to help you stay prepared?

-----------------------------------------------------------

-----------------------------------------------------------

-----------------------------------------------------------

-----------------------------------------------------------

-----------------------------------------------------------

-----------------------------------------------------------

6. Reflect on a time when you felt unprepared. What steps could you have taken to better equip yourself for that situation?

-----------------------------------------------------------

-----------------------------------------------------------

-----------------------------------------------------------

-----------------------------------------------------------

-----------------------------------------------------------

-----------------------------------------------------------

7. How can you and your friends foster a culture of

preparedness in your social circles or communities?

------------------------------------------------
------------------------------------------------
------------------------------------------------
------------------------------------------------
------------------------------------------------
------------------------------------------------

8. In what ways has being prepared positively impacted your decision-making and problem-solving skills?

------------------------------------------------
------------------------------------------------
------------------------------------------------
------------------------------------------------
------------------------------------------------
------------------------------------------------

9. How do you and your peers stay adaptable when

faced with unexpected changes to plans or circumstances?

---

---

---

---

---

---

10. Consider your current goals and aspirations. How can you and your support network help you be better prepared for the challenges that may arise on your journey?

---

---

---

---

---

---

## Ask for help from others:

# Key lesson

1. Recognizing the Importance of Seeking Help: Understand the significance of asking for help when facing challenges or difficult situations.
2. Building a Support System: Learn how to identify trustworthy individuals who can provide guidance and support in times of need.
3. Developing Effective Communication Skills: Acquire the skills to express your thoughts and emotions clearly when seeking assistance from others.
4. Overcoming Pride and Fear: Explore the idea that asking for help is a sign of strength, overcoming any reluctance driven by pride or fear.
5. Reciprocity and Community: Recognize the value of offering help to others, fostering a sense of community where assistance is a two-way street.

# Reflection Questions

1. How have you demonstrated the importance of seeking help in your own life recently?

-----------------------------------------------------------

-----------------------------------------------------------

-----------------------------------------------------------

-----------------------------------------------------------

----------------------------------------------------------------

----------------------------------------------------------------

2. Can you identify three people in your life whom you consider reliable sources of support and guidance?

----------------------------------------------------------------

----------------------------------------------------------------

----------------------------------------------------------------

----------------------------------------------------------------

----------------------------------------------------------------

----------------------------------------------------------------

3. In what ways do you communicate effectively when asking for help, ensuring your needs and concerns are clearly understood?

----------------------------------------------------------------

----------------------------------------------------------------

----------------------------------------------------------------

----------------------------------------------------------------

----------------------------------------------------------------

----------------------------------------------------------------

4. Reflect on a situation where pride or fear hindered you from seeking help. How did you overcome these barriers, or what steps could you take in the future?

------------------------------------------------------------

------------------------------------------------------------

------------------------------------------------------------

------------------------------------------------------------

------------------------------------------------------------

------------------------------------------------------------

5. Share an experience where you offered help to someone else. How did this contribute to building a sense of community?

------------------------------------------------------------

------------------------------------------------------------

------------------------------------------------------------

------------------------------------------------------------

------------------------------------------------------------

------------------------------------------------------------

6. Are there specific areas in your life where you find it challenging to ask for help? Why do you think that is, and how can you address those challenges?

-------------------------------------------------------------

-------------------------------------------------------------

-------------------------------------------------------------

-------------------------------------------------------------

-------------------------------------------------------------

-------------------------------------------------------------

7. Consider a time when you asked for help and received valuable assistance. How did this experience impact your perspective on seeking help?

-------------------------------------------------------------

-------------------------------------------------------------

-------------------------------------------------------------

-------------------------------------------------------------

-------------------------------------------------------------

------------------------------------------------------------

8. Who are the people in your life that you can turn to for emotional support, and how do you nurture those relationships?

------------------------------------------------------------

------------------------------------------------------------

------------------------------------------------------------

------------------------------------------------------------

------------------------------------------------------------

------------------------------------------------------------

9. Reflect on the balance between self-reliance and seeking help. How can you strike a healthy balance between independence and reaching out to others?

------------------------------------------------------------

------------------------------------------------------------

------------------------------------------------------------

------------------------------------------------------------

------------------------------------------------------------

------------------------------------------------------------

10. Think about a situation where asking for help led to a positive outcome. How can you apply the lessons learned from that experience in future challenges?

------------------------------------------------------------

------------------------------------------------------------

------------------------------------------------------------

------------------------------------------------------------

------------------------------------------------------------

------------------------------------------------------------

## Five "Tricks" to help you track your progress:

## Key Lessons

1. Setting Clear Goals: Establish specific and achievable goals that you can work towards. Clear objectives help you measure progress and stay motivated.

2. Consistent Self-Monitoring: Regularly monitor your behavior and actions to assess whether you're aligning with your goals. Consistency is key to making positive changes.

3. Celebrate Small Wins: Acknowledge and celebrate your achievements, no matter how small. Recognizing progress boosts morale and encourages continued effort.

4. Adaptability and Flexibility: Be willing to adjust your goals and strategies based on your experiences. Flexibility is crucial for long-term success in behavior improvement.

5. Seeking Support: Don't hesitate to reach out for support from friends, family, or mentors. Having a support system can provide guidance, encouragement, and accountability.

## Reflection Questions

1. How have your goal-setting practices evolved since incorporating the techniques from Chapter 5 into your routine?

------------------------------------------------------------

------------------------------------------------------------

------------------------------------------------------------

------------------------------------------------------------

------------------------------------------------------------

------------------------------------------------------------

2. Can you identify specific instances where

consistent self-monitoring has helped you make better choices in challenging situations?

----------------------------------------------------------------

----------------------------------------------------------------

----------------------------------------------------------------

----------------------------------------------------------------

----------------------------------------------------------------

----------------------------------------------------------------

3. Reflect on a recent accomplishment, no matter how small. How did acknowledging this achievement impact your motivation to continue working on your behavior?

----------------------------------------------------------------

----------------------------------------------------------------

----------------------------------------------------------------

----------------------------------------------------------------

----------------------------------------------------------------

----------------------------------------------------------------

4. In what ways have you demonstrated

adaptability and flexibility in adjusting your goals based on your experiences and progress?

-----------------------------------------------------------

-----------------------------------------------------------

-----------------------------------------------------------

-----------------------------------------------------------

-----------------------------------------------------------

-----------------------------------------------------------

5. Who in your life has been a valuable source of support as you work on improving your behavior? How have they contributed to your progress?

-----------------------------------------------------------

-----------------------------------------------------------

-----------------------------------------------------------

-----------------------------------------------------------

-----------------------------------------------------------

-----------------------------------------------------------

6. Have you encountered any unexpected challenges while implementing the tracking

techniques? How did you overcome or adapt to these challenges?

------------------------------------------------

------------------------------------------------

------------------------------------------------

------------------------------------------------

------------------------------------------------

------------------------------------------------

7. Consider a time when you faced setbacks in your behavior improvement journey. How did you bounce back, and what did you learn from those setbacks?

------------------------------------------------

------------------------------------------------

------------------------------------------------

------------------------------------------------

------------------------------------------------

------------------------------------------------

8. How do you prioritize and manage your time

effectively to ensure consistent progress tracking without feeling overwhelmed?

---------------------------------------------------------------

---------------------------------------------------------------

---------------------------------------------------------------

---------------------------------------------------------------

---------------------------------------------------------------

---------------------------------------------------------------

9. Are there specific tricks or strategies from Chapter 5 that you find particularly effective? How do they align with your strengths and preferences?

---------------------------------------------------------------

---------------------------------------------------------------

---------------------------------------------------------------

---------------------------------------------------------------

---------------------------------------------------------------

---------------------------------------------------------------

10. Reflect on your overall experience using the tracking methods outlined in the chapter. How has

this impacted not only your behavior but also your mindset and outlook on personal growth?

-----------------------------------------------------------

-----------------------------------------------------------

-----------------------------------------------------------

-----------------------------------------------------------

-----------------------------------------------------------

-----------------------------------------------------------

## Ways to Get Along Better with Teachers:

## Say Nice Things to Teachers
## Key Lessons

1. Building Positive Relationships:
   - Teachers play a crucial role in your educational journey. Expressing gratitude and kindness can foster a positive relationship with them.
2. Effective Communication:
   - Learning to communicate positively with teachers helps create a supportive and collaborative learning environment.
3. Understanding Perspectives:
   - Recognize that teachers have unique challenges and perspectives. Showing empathy and

understanding can lead to more productive interactions.

4. Promoting a Positive Classroom Atmosphere:

- Your words contribute to the overall classroom atmosphere. Saying nice things can create a more enjoyable and conducive learning environment for everyone.

5. Advocating for Yourself:

- Expressing appreciation and respect for your teachers can positively impact your educational experience and help you advocate for your needs.

## Reflection Questions

1. How can you incorporate more positive language when interacting with your teachers?

------------------------------------------------------------

------------------------------------------------------------

------------------------------------------------------------

------------------------------------------------------------

------------------------------------------------------------

------------------------------------------------------------

2. In what ways do you currently express gratitude or appreciation towards your teachers?

---------------------------------------------------------

---------------------------------------------------------

---------------------------------------------------------

---------------------------------------------------------

---------------------------------------------------------

---------------------------------------------------------

3. How does saying nice things to your teachers contribute to a better classroom atmosphere for everyone?

---------------------------------------------------------

---------------------------------------------------------

---------------------------------------------------------

---------------------------------------------------------

---------------------------------------------------------

---------------------------------------------------------

-4. Reflect on a specific instance where positive communication with a teacher had a positive impact on your learning experience.

---------------------------------------------------

---------------------------------------------------

---------------------------------------------------

---------------------------------------------------

---------------------------------------------------

---------------------------------------------------

5. How can you be more mindful of the challenges and perspectives that your teachers may face in their roles?

---------------------------------------------------

---------------------------------------------------

---------------------------------------------------

---------------------------------------------------

---------------------------------------------------

---------------------------------------------------

6. Consider the role of positive communication in building a supportive educational community. How can you actively contribute to this community?

---------------------------------------------------------

---------------------------------------------------------

---------------------------------------------------------

---------------------------------------------------------

---------------------------------------------------------

---------------------------------------------------------

7. Reflect on the importance of effective communication in addressing any concerns or challenges you may have in your educational journey.

---------------------------------------------------------

---------------------------------------------------------

---------------------------------------------------------

---------------------------------------------------------

---------------------------------------------------------

---------------------------------------------------------

8. How can expressing kindness towards your teachers positively influence your overall attitude towards school?

---------------------------------------------------------

---------------------------------------------------------

---------------------------------------------------------

---------------------------------------------------------

---------------------------------------------------------

---------------------------------------------------------

9. Consider the difference between constructive feedback and criticism. How can you ensure your communication with teachers is constructive?

---------------------------------------------------------

---------------------------------------------------------

---------------------------------------------------------

---------------------------------------------------------

---------------------------------------------------------

---------------------------------------------------------

10. Reflect on the link between expressing gratitude to teachers and advocating for your own needs in the educational setting.

---------------------------------------------------------

---------------------------------------------------------

---------------------------------------------------------

---------------------------------------------------------

---------------------------------------------------------

---------------------------------------------------------

## Let Teachers Teach:

## Key Lessons

1. Empowerment of Educators: Recognize the importance of allowing teachers the autonomy to implement effective teaching strategies without unnecessary interference.

2. Trust in Professionalism: Understand the significance of trusting teachers' professional judgment and expertise in managing their classrooms.

3. Effective Classroom Management: Emphasize the need for teachers to have the freedom to establish and maintain a positive learning environment through appropriate disciplinary measures.

4. Tailoring Teaching Methods: Acknowledge the diversity of teaching styles and methods and

encourage educators to use what works best for their students.

5. Promoting Student Success: Highlight the connection between teacher autonomy and student success, emphasizing the role teachers play in fostering a conducive learning atmosphere.

## Reflection Questions

1. How do you perceive the balance between giving teacher autonomy and ensuring accountability for student outcomes?

------------------------------------------------------------

------------------------------------------------------------

------------------------------------------------------------

------------------------------------------------------------

------------------------------------------------------------

------------------------------------------------------------

2. In what ways can a trusting relationship between school administration and teachers positively impact the overall school climate and student performance?

---------------------------------------------------

---------------------------------------------------

---------------------------------------------------

---------------------------------------------------

---------------------------------------------------

---------------------------------------------------

3. Reflect on a time when a teacher's autonomy positively influenced your learning experience. What aspects made it effective?

---------------------------------------------------

---------------------------------------------------

---------------------------------------------------

---------------------------------------------------

---------------------------------------------------

---------------------------------------------------

4. Consider the challenges teachers may face when not granted sufficient autonomy in the classroom. How can these challenges impact both teachers and students?

------------------------------------------------------------

------------------------------------------------------------

------------------------------------------------------------

------------------------------------------------------------

------------------------------------------------------------

------------------------------------------------------------

5. How can a school system ensure that teachers have the necessary support and resources to exercise their professional judgment effectively?

------------------------------------------------------------

------------------------------------------------------------

------------------------------------------------------------

------------------------------------------------------------

------------------------------------------------------------

------------------------------------------------------------

6. Reflect on the relationship between teacher autonomy and student engagement. How does teacher empowerment contribute to a more engaging learning environment?

------------------------------------------------------------

------------------------------------------------------------

------------------------------------------------------------

------------------------------------------------------------

------------------------------------------------------------

------------------------------------------------------------

7. In what ways can a standardized approach to teaching hinder the creativity and adaptability of educators?

------------------------------------------------------------

------------------------------------------------------------

------------------------------------------------------------

------------------------------------------------------------

------------------------------------------------------------

------------------------------------------------------------

8. Consider the role of trust in fostering a positive teacher-student relationship. How can a trusting environment contribute to better behavioral outcomes?

-------------------------------------------------------

-------------------------------------------------------

-------------------------------------------------------

-------------------------------------------------------

-------------------------------------------------------

-------------------------------------------------------

9. Reflect on the impact of teacher empowerment on school culture. How does a supportive environment for teachers influence the overall morale of the school community?

-------------------------------------------------------

-------------------------------------------------------

-------------------------------------------------------

-------------------------------------------------------

-------------------------------------------------------

-------------------------------------------------------

10. How can school administrators strike a balance between providing guidelines for classroom management and allowing teachers the flexibility

to tailor strategies to their unique classroom dynamics?

-----------------------------------------------------------
-----------------------------------------------------------
-----------------------------------------------------------
-----------------------------------------------------------
-----------------------------------------------------------
-----------------------------------------------------------

## Make suggestions with questions:

### Key Lessons

1. Empowerment through Inquiry:
Encourage a mindset of empowerment by demonstrating the effectiveness of making suggestions through thoughtful questions.
2. Active Engagement:
Foster active engagement by emphasizing the importance of using questions as a tool for expressing suggestions, which invites participation and collaboration.
3. Developing Communication Skills:
Highlight the role of questioning in honing communication skills, and helping children articulate their thoughts and ideas effectively.

4. Understanding Perspectives:

Illustrate how making suggestions with questions promotes an understanding of different perspectives, fostering empathy and cooperative problem-solving.

5. Conflict Resolution:

Teach the value of questions in resolving conflicts by facilitating open dialogue and creating an environment where conflicts can be addressed constructively.

## Reflection Questions

1. How can you apply the concept of making suggestions through questions in your daily interactions with peers and adults?

---------------------------------------------------------------

---------------------------------------------------------------

---------------------------------------------------------------

---------------------------------------------------------------

---------------------------------------------------------------

---------------------------------------------------------------

2. Consider a recent situation where you had a suggestion. How might framing it as a question have influenced the outcome?

---------------------------------------------------------------

---------------------------------------------------------------

---------------------------------------------------------------

---------------------------------------------------------------

---------------------------------------------------------------

---------------------------------------------------------------

3. In what ways do you think using questions to make suggestions can positively impact your communication with friends and family?

---------------------------------------------------------------

---------------------------------------------------------------

---------------------------------------------------------------

---------------------------------------------------------------

---------------------------------------------------------------

---------------------------------------------------------------

4. Reflect on a time when someone suggested that you use questions. How did it make you feel, and what did you learn from that experience?

------------------------------------------------------------

------------------------------------------------------------

------------------------------------------------------------

------------------------------------------------------------

------------------------------------------------------------

------------------------------------------------------------

5. How can you adapt your approach to suggesting ideas to ensure they are more collaborative and invite others to share their thoughts?

------------------------------------------------------------

------------------------------------------------------------

------------------------------------------------------------

------------------------------------------------------------

------------------------------------------------------------

------------------------------------------------------------

6. Think about a current challenge you are facing. How might posing questions help you brainstorm solutions and seek support from others?

---------------------------------------------------

---------------------------------------------------

---------------------------------------------------

---------------------------------------------------

---------------------------------------------------

---------------------------------------------------

7. Consider the role of questions in understanding someone else's perspective. How might this approach improve your relationships with friends or family members?

---------------------------------------------------

---------------------------------------------------

---------------------------------------------------

---------------------------------------------------

---------------------------------------------------

---------------------------------------------------

8. Reflect on the connection between effective communication and making suggestions with questions. How can this skill contribute to your success in different areas of your life?

---------------------------------------------------------

---------------------------------------------------------

---------------------------------------------------------

---------------------------------------------------------

---------------------------------------------------------

---------------------------------------------------------

9. In what ways can incorporating questions into your suggestions help you navigate and resolve conflicts with others?

10. Imagine a group project or activity. How can you use questions to facilitate collaboration and ensure everyone's ideas are considered?

---------------------------------------------------------

---------------------------------------------------------

---------------------------------------------------------

---------------------------------------------------------

---------------------------------------------------------

---------------------------------------------------------

## Make a sandwich:

# Key Lessons

1. The Art of Decision-Making:
Understanding the process of making a sandwich serves as a metaphor for decision-making. Learn how to assess options, make choices, and navigate through the consequences.

2. Building Independence:
Making a sandwich requires a series of sequential steps. Through this process, you'll discover the importance of independence and self-reliance in completing tasks successfully.

3. Time Management:
Crafting a sandwich efficiently involves managing your time wisely. Explore the connection between time management skills and accomplishing daily tasks without feeling overwhelmed.

4. Responsibility and Consequences:
Every ingredient you choose has an impact on the final product. Relate this to understanding responsibility and facing the consequences of your decisions, both positive and negative.

5. Adaptability and Creativity:
Experimenting with different ingredients and flavors encourages creativity. Apply this mindset to real-life situations, fostering adaptability and a willingness to explore new approaches.

## Reflection Questions

1. How did the process of making a sandwich teach you about decision-making in your daily life?

------------------------------------------------------------

------------------------------------------------------------

------------------------------------------------------------

------------------------------------------------------------

------------------------------------------------------------

------------------------------------------------------------

2. In what ways did building a sandwich foster a sense of independence, and how can you apply this independence to other aspects of your life?

------------------------------------------------------------

------------------------------------------------------------

------------------------------------------------------------

------------------------------------------------------------

------------------------------------------------------------

------------------------------------------------------------

3. Reflect on the time management skills you utilized while making a sandwich. How can you

implement similar strategies in your schoolwork or other activities?

------------------------------------------------------------

------------------------------------------------------------

------------------------------------------------------------

------------------------------------------------------------

------------------------------------------------------------

------------------------------------------------------------

4. Consider the responsibility involved in choosing ingredients for your sandwich. How does this relate to being responsible in your interactions with friends, family, and your commitments?

------------------------------------------------------------

------------------------------------------------------------

------------------------------------------------------------

------------------------------------------------------------

------------------------------------------------------------

------------------------------------------------------------

5. What were the consequences, both positive and

negative, of the choices you made while making a sandwich? How can you use this awareness to make better decisions in the future?

-------------------------------------------------------------

-------------------------------------------------------------

-------------------------------------------------------------

-------------------------------------------------------------

-------------------------------------------------------------

-------------------------------------------------------------

6. Discuss how the step-by-step process of making a sandwich helped you develop a systematic approach to tasks. How can you transfer this skill to improve your efficiency in daily routines?

-------------------------------------------------------------

-------------------------------------------------------------

-------------------------------------------------------------

-------------------------------------------------------------

-------------------------------------------------------------

-------------------------------------------------------------

7. Reflect on any challenges you faced while making a sandwich. How did you overcome these challenges, and what did you learn from the experience?

------------------------------------------------------------

------------------------------------------------------------

------------------------------------------------------------

------------------------------------------------------------

------------------------------------------------------------

------------------------------------------------------------

8. Explore the connection between trying new ingredients in a sandwich and being open to new ideas in your life. How can you embrace creativity and adaptability in various situations?

------------------------------------------------------------

------------------------------------------------------------

------------------------------------------------------------

------------------------------------------------------------

------------------------------------------------------------

---------------------------------------------------------------

9. Analyze the importance of teamwork if you made the sandwich with someone else. How can collaboration enhance your ability to achieve goals in other areas of your life?

---------------------------------------------------------------

---------------------------------------------------------------

---------------------------------------------------------------

---------------------------------------------------------------

---------------------------------------------------------------

---------------------------------------------------------------

10. Consider the sensory experience of making and eating a sandwich. How can mindfulness and awareness of your surroundings contribute to better decision-making in challenging situations?

---------------------------------------------------------------

---------------------------------------------------------------

---------------------------------------------------------------

---------------------------------------------------------------

---------------------------------------------------------------

---------------------------------------------------------------

## Use behavior mod:

## Key Lessons

1. Understanding Behavior Modification: In Chapter 6 of "The Survival Guide for Kids with Behavior Challenges," Thomas McIntyre introduces the concept of behavior modification. This lesson emphasizes the importance of recognizing and modifying behavior to make positive choices.

2. Identifying Triggers: Learn to identify triggers that lead to challenging behavior. By understanding what sets off negative reactions, you can proactively manage situations and make choices that lead to more positive outcomes.

3. Implementing Positive Reinforcement: Discover the power of positive reinforcement in shaping behavior. Chapter 6 guides you on how to use rewards and positive feedback to encourage good choices and discourage unwanted behavior.

4. Setting Realistic Goals: The chapter emphasizes the significance of setting achievable goals. By breaking down larger objectives into manageable tasks, you can create a roadmap for success, making it easier to stay on the path of positive behavior.

5. Developing Self-Awareness: Cultivate self-awareness by reflecting on your behavior and its impact on others. Through self-reflection, you gain insights into your actions, paving the way for personal growth and improved decision-making.

## Reflection Questions

1. How can you apply the principles of behavior modification in your daily life to make better choices?

-------------------------------------------------------------

-------------------------------------------------------------

-------------------------------------------------------------

-------------------------------------------------------------

-------------------------------------------------------------

-------------------------------------------------------------

2. Reflect on a recent situation where you exhibited challenging behavior. What triggered this behavior, and how could you modify it in the future?

-------------------------------------------------------------

-------------------------------------------------------------

-------------------------------------------------------------

---------------------------------------------------------
---------------------------------------------------------
---------------------------------------------------------

3. In what ways can positive reinforcement be incorporated into your routine to encourage positive behavior?

---------------------------------------------------------
---------------------------------------------------------
---------------------------------------------------------
---------------------------------------------------------
---------------------------------------------------------
---------------------------------------------------------

4. Consider a long-term goal you have. How can you break it down into smaller, more achievable steps using the principles discussed in Chapter 6?

---------------------------------------------------------
---------------------------------------------------------
---------------------------------------------------------
---------------------------------------------------------

---------------------------------------------------------------

---------------------------------------------------------------

5. Reflect on a time when you successfully modified your behavior. What strategies did you employ, and how can you apply them consistently?

---------------------------------------------------------------

---------------------------------------------------------------

---------------------------------------------------------------

---------------------------------------------------------------

---------------------------------------------------------------

---------------------------------------------------------------

6. Identify three potential triggers for negative behavior in your life. What proactive steps can you take to minimize their impact?

---------------------------------------------------------------

---------------------------------------------------------------

---------------------------------------------------------------

---------------------------------------------------------------

---------------------------------------------------------------

----------------------------------------------------------

7. How can you involve others in your behavior modification journey, such as family or friends, to provide support and encouragement?

----------------------------------------------------------

----------------------------------------------------------

----------------------------------------------------------

----------------------------------------------------------

----------------------------------------------------------

----------------------------------------------------------

8. Explore the role of self-awareness in making good choices. How does understanding your emotions and reactions contribute to better decision-making?

----------------------------------------------------------

----------------------------------------------------------

----------------------------------------------------------

----------------------------------------------------------

----------------------------------------------------------

----------------------------------------------------------

9. Consider a challenging situation where you maintained composure and made a positive choice. What strategies did you use to stay in control, and how can you replicate them?

------------------------------------------------------------

------------------------------------------------------------

------------------------------------------------------------

------------------------------------------------------------

------------------------------------------------------------

------------------------------------------------------------

10. Reflect on the impact of your behavior on those around you. How can you enhance your empathy and understanding of others' perspectives to improve relationships?

------------------------------------------------------------

------------------------------------------------------------

------------------------------------------------------------

------------------------------------------------------------

------------------------------------------------------------

------------------------------------------------------------

# Use your skills Together:

## Key Lessons

1. Collaborative Problem-Solving: The chapter emphasizes the importance of working together with others to solve problems. Learn how combining your skills with those of your peers can lead to more effective solutions.
2. Communication is Key: Explore the power of effective communication in building strong relationships. The chapter delves into how expressing yourself clearly and listening actively can foster better understanding and cooperation.
3. Teamwork and Synergy: Discover the concept of synergy, where the combined efforts of a group result in a more significant impact than individual efforts alone. Understand how your unique skills contribute to the collective success of a team.
4. Respecting Differences: Learn the art of appreciating diversity within a group. The chapter highlights the value of respecting others' skills, perspectives, and backgrounds, creating a harmonious and productive collaborative environment.
5. Celebrating Success Together: Understand the importance of acknowledging and celebrating collective achievements. Discover how recognizing and celebrating the successes of the

team can strengthen bonds and motivate everyone to continue working together.

## Reflection Questions

1. How can you leverage your unique skills to complement those of your peers in a group setting?

-----------------------------------------------------------

-----------------------------------------------------------

-----------------------------------------------------------

-----------------------------------------------------------

-----------------------------------------------------------

-----------------------------------------------------------

2. Reflect on a recent situation where effective communication played a crucial role. What strategies did you use, and how could you improve your communication skills further?

-----------------------------------------------------------

-----------------------------------------------------------

-----------------------------------------------------------

-----------------------------------------------------------

-----------------------------------------------------------

---------------------------------------------------------------

3. Think about a successful team you've been a part of. What specific contributions did you make, and how did your skills enhance the overall performance of the team?

---------------------------------------------------------------

---------------------------------------------------------------

---------------------------------------------------------------

---------------------------------------------------------------

---------------------------------------------------------------

---------------------------------------------------------------

4. In what ways can you actively demonstrate respect for the diverse skills, opinions, and backgrounds of your peers?

---------------------------------------------------------------

---------------------------------------------------------------

---------------------------------------------------------------

---------------------------------------------------------------

---------------------------------------------------------------

-----------------------------------------------------------------

5. Share a specific example of a collaborative success. What role did each team member play, and how did the combined efforts lead to a positive outcome?

-----------------------------------------------------------------

-----------------------------------------------------------------

-----------------------------------------------------------------

-----------------------------------------------------------------

-----------------------------------------------------------------

-----------------------------------------------------------------

6. How do you handle disagreements within a group? Reflect on a situation where differences arose and consider alternative approaches for resolving conflicts constructively.

-----------------------------------------------------------------

-----------------------------------------------------------------

-----------------------------------------------------------------

-----------------------------------------------------------------

---------------------------------------------------------------

---------------------------------------------------------------

7. Identify a challenge you've faced recently and brainstorm ways in which collaborating with others could have enhanced the problem-solving process.

---------------------------------------------------------------

---------------------------------------------------------------

---------------------------------------------------------------

---------------------------------------------------------------

---------------------------------------------------------------

---------------------------------------------------------------

8. Reflect on the impact of teamwork on your personal growth. How has collaborating with others contributed to your development and learning?

---------------------------------------------------------------

---------------------------------------------------------------

---------------------------------------------------------------

---------------------------------------------------------------

---------------------------------------------------------------

---------------------------------------------------------------

9. Consider a situation where you may have underestimated the importance of collective effort. What would you do differently now to ensure better collaboration?

---------------------------------------------------------------

---------------------------------------------------------------

---------------------------------------------------------------

---------------------------------------------------------------

---------------------------------------------------------------

---------------------------------------------------------------

10. Reflect on the role of celebration in teamwork. How can you actively participate in acknowledging and celebrating achievements within your group?

---------------------------------------------------------------

---------------------------------------------------------------

---------------------------------------------------------------

---------------------------------------------------------

---------------------------------------------------------

---------------------------------------------------------

# Ways to make and keep friends

## Say nice things to others:
## Key Lessons

1. The Power of Positivity:
   In this chapter, the importance of speaking kindly to others is emphasized. Saying nice things not only makes others feel good but also contributes to a positive and supportive environment.

2. Building Relationships:
   Lesson two delves into how expressing kindness through words fosters stronger connections with peers, family, and teachers. Positive communication is a key element in building and maintaining healthy relationships.

3. Empathy and Understanding:
   Saying nice things involves understanding others' perspectives and feelings. This chapter explores the concept of empathy, encouraging you to put yourself in others' shoes before speaking and to consider how your words might impact them

4. Creating a Positive Atmosphere:

The chapter highlights the role of individuals in shaping the atmosphere around them. By choosing positive words, you contribute to a more uplifting and harmonious environment for everyone.

5. Resolving Conflicts through Communication:

Effective communication is crucial in conflict resolution. This lesson explores how saying nice things can be a powerful tool in resolving conflicts and finding peaceful solutions.

## Reflection Questions

1. How can incorporating positive words into your daily interactions improve your relationships with family and friends?

-------------------------------------------------------

-------------------------------------------------------

-------------------------------------------------------

-------------------------------------------------------

-------------------------------------------------------

-------------------------------------------------------

2. Reflect on a recent situation where you chose to say something nice. How did it impact the atmosphere of the conversation or the overall environment?

---------------------------------------------------------------
---------------------------------------------------------------
---------------------------------------------------------------
---------------------------------------------------------------
---------------------------------------------------------------
---------------------------------------------------------------

3. In what ways can expressing kindness through words contribute to a more supportive and inclusive community at school?

---------------------------------------------------------------
---------------------------------------------------------------
---------------------------------------------------------------
---------------------------------------------------------------
---------------------------------------------------------------
---------------------------------------------------------------

4. Consider a time when you received a compliment. How did it make you feel, and how can you replicate that positive experience for others?

----------------------------------------

----------------------------------------

----------------------------------------

----------------------------------------

----------------------------------------

----------------------------------------

5. How can empathy play a role in choosing your words when communicating with others?

----------------------------------------

----------------------------------------

----------------------------------------

----------------------------------------

----------------------------------------

----------------------------------------

6. Reflect on a challenging situation where saying something nice could have diffused tension. What words could you have used to positively influence the outcome?

----------------------------------------

----------------------------------------

----------------------------------------

---------------------------------------------------------------

---------------------------------------------------------------

---------------------------------------------------------------

7. How can incorporating positive affirmations into your self-talk enhance your overall well-being and confidence?

---------------------------------------------------------------

---------------------------------------------------------------

---------------------------------------------------------------

---------------------------------------------------------------

---------------------------------------------------------------

8. Think about a peer who may be facing difficulties. How can your words provide support and encouragement during their tough times?

---------------------------------------------------------------

---------------------------------------------------------------

---------------------------------------------------------------

---------------------------------------------------------------

---------------------------------------------------------------

---------------------------------------------------------------

9. In what ways can saying nice things contribute to a more positive and productive learning environment in your classroom?

10. Reflect on the concept of "think before you speak." How can this practice help you avoid unintentionally hurting others with your words and contribute to a more positive social atmosphere?

---------------------------------------------------------------

---------------------------------------------------------------

---------------------------------------------------------------

---------------------------------------------------------------

---------------------------------------------------------------

---------------------------------------------------------------

## Ask people about themselves

In the seventh chapter of "The Survival Guide for Kids with Behavior Challenges: How to Make Good Choices and Stay out of Trouble," author Thomas McIntyre explores the valuable skill of asking people about themselves. This crucial social skill not only helps in building positive relationships but also contributes to personal growth. Here are five key lessons from the chapter along with ten reflection questions:

## Key Lessons

1. Building Connections: Asking people about themselves is a powerful tool for building connections. It shows genuine interest and helps create a sense of camaraderie.
2. Empathy and Understanding: By asking about others, you develop empathy and understanding. This skill fosters a positive environment and strengthens your ability to relate to different perspectives.
3. Effective Communication: Asking questions is a key component of effective communication. It encourages a two-way dialogue, making interactions more meaningful and engaging.
4. Personal Growth: Learning about others contributes to your personal growth. It broadens your knowledge, enhances your social skills, and provides valuable insights into diverse experiences.
5. Conflict Resolution: Understanding others through thoughtful questions can prevent and resolve conflicts. It promotes open communication, reducing misunderstandings and fostering a harmonious environment.

## Reflection Questions

1. How can regularly asking people about themselves enhance your ability to build lasting connections?

-------------------------------------------------------

-------------------------------------------------------

-------------------------------------------------------

-------------------------------------------------------

-------------------------------------------------------

-------------------------------------------------------

2. In what ways does asking questions contribute to the development of empathy and a deeper understanding of others?

-------------------------------------------------------

-------------------------------------------------------

-------------------------------------------------------

-------------------------------------------------------

-------------------------------------------------------

-------------------------------------------------------

3. How can effective communication be improved by incorporating the habit of asking people about themselves?

---------------------------------------------------

---------------------------------------------------

---------------------------------------------------

---------------------------------------------------

---------------------------------------------------

---------------------------------------------------

4. Reflect on a recent experience where learning about someone else's perspective had a positive impact on your own growth?

---------------------------------------------------

---------------------------------------------------

---------------------------------------------------

---------------------------------------------------

---------------------------------------------------

---------------------------------------------------

5. Consider a situation where asking questions could have prevented a misunderstanding. How will you approach similar situations in the future?

------------------------------------------------

------------------------------------------------

------------------------------------------------

------------------------------------------------

------------------------------------------------

------------------------------------------------

6. How can the skill of asking about others be applied in your academic or professional life to create a more positive and collaborative environment?

------------------------------------------------

------------------------------------------------

------------------------------------------------

------------------------------------------------

------------------------------------------------

------------------------------------------------

7. Reflect on a time when you felt truly heard and understood. What role did asking questions play in that experience?

---------------------------------------------

---------------------------------------------

---------------------------------------------

---------------------------------------------

---------------------------------------------

---------------------------------------------

8. In what ways does asking people about themselves align with the values of respect and consideration in your relationships?

---------------------------------------------

---------------------------------------------

---------------------------------------------

---------------------------------------------

---------------------------------------------

---------------------------------------------

9. Explore how the habit of asking questions can be utilized as a proactive approach to conflict resolution.

---------------------------------------------------------------

---------------------------------------------------------------

---------------------------------------------------------------

---------------------------------------------------------------

---------------------------------------------------------------

---------------------------------------------------------------

10. Think about a goal you have, and consider how asking for advice or insights from others can contribute to your success.

---------------------------------------------------------------

---------------------------------------------------------------

---------------------------------------------------------------

---------------------------------------------------------------

---------------------------------------------------------------

---------------------------------------------------------------

## Give a helping hand:

## Key Lessons

1. The Power of Empathy:

In this chapter, you'll discover the profound impact that showing empathy can have on your relationships. Learn how understanding and sharing the feelings of others can foster compassion and connection.

2. Community Building:

"Give a Helping Hand" emphasizes the importance of building a supportive community. Explore how contributing to the well-being of others not only strengthens your community but also enriches your own life.

3. Problem-Solving Skills:

Delve into effective problem-solving strategies as outlined in this chapter. Understanding how to approach challenges with a positive mindset and a willingness to help others can lead to mutually beneficial solutions.

4. Responsibility and Accountability:

Take a closer look at the concepts of responsibility and accountability. Discover how your actions can positively or negatively affect those around you, and learn ways to take ownership of your behavior.

5. Long-Term Benefits of Helping Others:

Explore the long-term benefits of giving a helping hand. Understand how being supportive and kind can contribute to a positive and inclusive environment, creating a better overall experience for everyone involved.

## Reflection Questions

1. How have you demonstrated empathy towards others in your life, and what impact did it have on your relationships?

---------------------------------------------------------

---------------------------------------------------------

---------------------------------------------------------

---------------------------------------------------------

---------------------------------------------------------

---------------------------------------------------------

2. Reflect on a specific instance where you actively contributed to building a supportive community. How did it make you feel, and what changes did you observe in the community?

---------------------------------------------------------

---------------------------------------------------------

---------------------------------------------------------

---------------------------------------------------------

---------------------------------------------------------

---------------------------------------------------------

3. Share a problem-solving experience from your

life where helping others played a crucial role. What strategies did you use, and what was the outcome?

-------------------------------------------------------------

-------------------------------------------------------------

-------------------------------------------------------------

-------------------------------------------------------------

-------------------------------------------------------------

-------------------------------------------------------------

4. In what ways do you currently practice responsibility and accountability in your daily interactions with others?

-------------------------------------------------------------

-------------------------------------------------------------

-------------------------------------------------------------

-------------------------------------------------------------

-------------------------------------------------------------

-------------------------------------------------------------

5. Consider the ripple effect of your actions on the

people around you. How can you ensure that your actions contribute positively to your immediate environment?

-------------------------------------------------------

-------------------------------------------------------

-------------------------------------------------------

-------------------------------------------------------

-------------------------------------------------------

-------------------------------------------------------

6. Reflect on a time when someone extended a helping hand to you. How did it impact your perspective, and did it inspire you to help others in return?

-------------------------------------------------------

-------------------------------------------------------

-------------------------------------------------------

-------------------------------------------------------

-------------------------------------------------------

-------------------------------------------------------

7. Think about a challenge you're currently facing. How might seeking help and collaborating with others lead to a more effective solution?

------------------------------------------------------------

------------------------------------------------------------

------------------------------------------------------------

------------------------------------------------------------

------------------------------------------------------------

------------------------------------------------------------

8. Explore the idea of long-term benefits in helping others. How can consistent acts of kindness contribute to a positive and inclusive environment over time?

------------------------------------------------------------

------------------------------------------------------------

------------------------------------------------------------

------------------------------------------------------------

------------------------------------------------------------

------------------------------------------------------------

9. Consider the concept of reciprocity in relationships. How does giving support to others create a cycle of positive interactions and mutual assistance?

----------------------------------------------------------------

----------------------------------------------------------------

----------------------------------------------------------------

----------------------------------------------------------------

----------------------------------------------------------------

----------------------------------------------------------------

10. Reflect on the role of empathy in conflict resolution. How can understanding others' perspectives help in finding common ground and resolving disputes?

----------------------------------------------------------------

----------------------------------------------------------------

----------------------------------------------------------------

----------------------------------------------------------------

----------------------------------------------------------------

---------------------------------------------------------------

# Take part in activities:

## Key Lessons

1. Explore Your Interests: Engaging in activities allows you to discover your passions and interests. Take the time to explore different hobbies and find what resonates with you.
2. Build Social Skills: Participating in group activities provides an opportunity to develop and enhance your social skills. Learning how to communicate effectively and work with others is a crucial life skill.
3. Time Management: Balancing school, chores, and activities can be challenging. Chapter 7 emphasizes the importance of managing your time wisely to ensure you can enjoy activities without neglecting other responsibilities.
4. Positive Outlet for Energy: Being part of activities offers a positive outlet for your energy. Instead of letting negative emotions build up, engaging in constructive activities helps channel your energy productively and healthily.
5. Sense of Achievement: Taking part in activities allows you to set goals and experience a sense of achievement when you accomplish them. This can boost your confidence and motivation in various aspects of life.

# Reflection Questions

1. What activities genuinely spark your interest, and how can you incorporate them into your routine?

------------------------------------------------------------

------------------------------------------------------------

------------------------------------------------------------

------------------------------------------------------------

------------------------------------------------------------

------------------------------------------------------------

2. How do you currently approach teamwork and collaboration in group activities, and what improvements could you make?

------------------------------------------------------------

------------------------------------------------------------

------------------------------------------------------------

------------------------------------------------------------

------------------------------------------------------------

------------------------------------------------------------

3. In what ways do your current time management habits support or hinder your ability to participate in activities?

------------------------------------------------------------

------------------------------------------------------------

------------------------------------------------------------

------------------------------------------------------------

------------------------------------------------------------

------------------------------------------------------------

4. Reflect on an activity that brought you joy. What specific elements of that activity contributed to your happiness?

------------------------------------------------------------

------------------------------------------------------------

------------------------------------------------------------

------------------------------------------------------------

------------------------------------------------------------

------------------------------------------------------------

5. Consider the balance between your academic

responsibilities and extracurricular activities. How can you ensure both aspects of your life receive adequate attention?

-------------------------------------------------------------

-------------------------------------------------------------

-------------------------------------------------------------

-------------------------------------------------------------

-------------------------------------------------------------

-------------------------------------------------------------

6. What strategies can you implement to use activities as a positive outlet for stress and frustration?

-------------------------------------------------------------

-------------------------------------------------------------

-------------------------------------------------------------

-------------------------------------------------------------

-------------------------------------------------------------

-------------------------------------------------------------

7. Think about a recent accomplishment in an

activity. How did it make you feel, and what lessons did you learn from the experience?

------------------------------------------------------------

------------------------------------------------------------

------------------------------------------------------------

------------------------------------------------------------

------------------------------------------------------------

------------------------------------------------------------

8. Are there any activities you've been hesitant to try? What steps can you take to overcome any fears or reservations?

9. Examine your current social circle. How can participating in new activities help you expand your network and build stronger connections?

10. Consider your long-term goals. How can the lessons learned from participating in activities contribute to your personal and professional development?

------------------------------------------------------------

------------------------------------------------------------

----------------------------------------------------------

----------------------------------------------------------

----------------------------------------------------------

----------------------------------------------------------

## Choose friends carefully:

## Key Lessons

1. Influence Matters: The people you surround yourself with have a significant impact on your behavior and choices. Choosing friends who make positive choices can greatly influence your decision-making.
2. Values Alignment: Select friends who share similar values and principles. Being surrounded by individuals who prioritize similar things as you can foster a supportive and understanding social circle.
3. Peer Pressure Awareness: Recognize the influence of peer pressure and the importance of resisting negative influences. Learning to say "no" when necessary helps you stay true to your values and goals.
4. Healthy Boundaries: Establishing clear boundaries with friends is crucial. Understanding your limits and communicating them respectfully contributes to the development of healthy relationships.

5. Evaluate Friendships: Regularly assess your friendships and their impact on your well-being. If a friendship consistently brings negativity or encourages poor choices, consider whether it's worth maintaining.

## Reflection Questions

1. How do the friends you choose reflect your values and priorities?

-------------------------------------------------------

-------------------------------------------------------

-------------------------------------------------------

-------------------------------------------------------

-------------------------------------------------------

-------------------------------------------------------

2. In what ways have your friends positively influenced your behavior and choices?

-------------------------------------------------------

-------------------------------------------------------

-------------------------------------------------------

-------------------------------------------------------

-------------------------------------------------------

-------------------------------------------------------

3. Are there instances where peer pressure has affected your decision-making? How did you handle it?

---------------------------------------------------------------

---------------------------------------------------------------

---------------------------------------------------------------

---------------------------------------------------------------

---------------------------------------------------------------

---------------------------------------------------------------

4. What qualities do you look for in a friend, and how do these align with your values?

---------------------------------------------------------------

---------------------------------------------------------------

---------------------------------------------------------------

---------------------------------------------------------------

---------------------------------------------------------------

---------------------------------------------------------------

5. Reflect on a time when a friend supported you

in making a positive choice. How did it impact your life?

------------------------------------------------------------

------------------------------------------------------------

------------------------------------------------------------

------------------------------------------------------------

------------------------------------------------------------

------------------------------------------------------------

6. How can you effectively communicate your boundaries to your friends without jeopardizing the relationship?

------------------------------------------------------------

------------------------------------------------------------

------------------------------------------------------------

------------------------------------------------------------

------------------------------------------------------------

------------------------------------------------------------

7. Have you ever had to say "no" to a friend's suggestion or request? How did you navigate that situation?

----------------------------------------

----------------------------------------

----------------------------------------

----------------------------------------

----------------------------------------

----------------------------------------

8. Consider the impact of negative influences from friends on your behavior. What strategies can you employ to resist such influences?

----------------------------------------

----------------------------------------

----------------------------------------

----------------------------------------

----------------------------------------

9. Evaluate your current friendships. Are there any that may be hurting your choices or well-being?

----------------------------------------

----------------------------------------

---------------------------------------------------------------

---------------------------------------------------------------

---------------------------------------------------------------

---------------------------------------------------------------

---------------------------------------------------------------

---------------------------------------------------------------

---------------------------------------------------------------

----------------------------------------------10. What
steps can you take to build and nurture positive,
supportive friendships moving forward?

---------------------------------------------------------------

---------------------------------------------------------------

---------------------------------------------------------------

---------------------------------------------------------------

---------------------------------------------------------------

---------------------------------------------------------------

## Ways to help the adults at home help you:

## Use talking and listening skills
### Key Lessons

1. Effective Communication: The chapter emphasizes the importance of using talking and listening skills to communicate effectively. Learn how to express your thoughts and feelings clearly to avoid misunderstandings.

2. Empathy and Understanding: Develop the ability to listen actively and understand others' perspectives. Practicing empathy can strengthen your relationships and help you navigate social situations more successfully.

3. Conflict Resolution: Acquire skills for resolving conflicts through open communication. Discover strategies to express your needs and concerns while also being receptive to the concerns of others.

4. Building Positive Relationships: Use talking and listening skills to build positive relationships with peers, family, and teachers. Developing strong connections with others contributes to a supportive and enriching environment.

5. Self-Advocacy: Learn to advocate for yourself by effectively communicating your needs and preferences. This skill is essential for personal growth and achieving your goals.

## Reflection Questions

1. How have you demonstrated effective communication skills in your recent interactions?

------------------------------------------

------------------------------------------

------------------------------------------

------------------------------------------

------------------------------------------

------------------------------------------

2. Can you recall a situation where active listening helped you better understand someone else's point of view? How did it impact the outcome?

------------------------------------------

------------------------------------------

------------------------------------------

------------------------------------------

------------------------------------------

------------------------------------------

3. In what ways have you utilized talking and listening skills to resolve conflicts in your relationships?

---------------------------------------------------

---------------------------------------------------

---------------------------------------------------

---------------------------------------------------

---------------------------------------------------

---------------------------------------------------

4. Reflect on a positive relationship in your life. How have your communication skills contributed to the strength of that relationship?

---------------------------------------------------

---------------------------------------------------

---------------------------------------------------

---------------------------------------------------

---------------------------------------------------

---------------------------------------------------

5. Describe a time when you successfully advocated for yourself using effective communication. What did you learn from that experience?

------------------------------------------------------------

------------------------------------------------------------

------------------------------------------------------------

.
------------------------------------------------------------

------------------------------------------------------------

------------------------------------------------------------

6. Are there instances where you could have employed better listening skills to avoid misunderstandings?

------------------------------------------------------------

------------------------------------------------------------

------------------------------------------------------------

------------------------------------------------------------

------------------------------------------------------------

------------------------------------------------------------

7. Consider a recent disagreement. How might improve communication have prevented or minimized the conflict?

-------------------------------------------------------

-------------------------------------------------------

-------------------------------------------------------

-------------------------------------------------------

-------------------------------------------------------

-------------------------------------------------------

8. How do you express empathy towards others? Can you think of a specific example where your empathy made a difference in a relationship?

-------------------------------------------------------

-------------------------------------------------------

-------------------------------------------------------

-------------------------------------------------------

-------------------------------------------------------

-------------------------------------------------------

9. Reflect on a conversation where you felt heard and understood. What elements of communication contributed to that positive experience?

----------------------------------------

----------------------------------------

----------------------------------------

----------------------------------------

----------------------------------------

----------------------------------------

10. Think about a goal you're working towards. How can improved talking and listening skills help you in achieving that goal by enhancing your interactions with others?

----------------------------------------

----------------------------------------

----------------------------------------

----------------------------------------

----------------------------------------

----------------------------------------

## Ask for help with your goal:

## Key Lessons

1. Recognizing the Power of Collaboration:

In Chapter 8, "Ask for Help with Your Goal," the importance of collaboration and seeking assistance in achieving your goals is highlighted. Recognize that asking for help is a strength, not a weakness.

2. Building a Support Network:

Learn how to cultivate a supportive network of individuals who can contribute positively to your journey. Surrounding yourself with people who believe in your goals can significantly enhance your chances of success.

3. Effective Communication Skills:

The chapter emphasizes the significance of effective communication when seeking help. Develop the ability to clearly articulate your needs, challenges, and goals to others, fostering a deeper understanding and support.

4. Learning from Diverse Perspectives:

Asking for help exposes you to a variety of perspectives and experiences. Embrace the opportunity to learn from others, gaining valuable insights that can contribute to your personal and professional growth.

5. Building Confidence through Collaboration:

By seeking help, you not only achieve your goals more efficiently but also build confidence in your ability to navigate challenges. Recognize that collaboration enhances both personal and collective
Success.

## Reflection Questions

1. How can you actively involve others in your goal-setting process to create a more collaborative and supportive environment for your aspirations?

------------------------------------------------------------

------------------------------------------------------------

------------------------------------------------------------

------------------------------------------------------------

------------------------------------------------------------

------------------------------------------------------------

2. Identify two individuals in your life whom you can approach for guidance regarding your goals. What qualities make them suitable mentors or advisors for your journey?

------------------------------------------------------------

------------------------------------------------------------

------------------------------------------------------------

------------------------------------------------------------

------------------------------------------------------------

------------------------------------------------------------

3. Reflect on an experience where seeking help positively impacts your ability to achieve a goal. What lessons can you extract from that experience to apply to your current objectives?

-------------------------------------------------------------

-------------------------------------------------------------

-------------------------------------------------------------

-------------------------------------------------------------

-------------------------------------------------------------

4. In what ways can you enhance your communication skills to more effectively convey your goals and challenges when seeking assistance from others?

-------------------------------------------------------------

-------------------------------------------------------------

-------------------------------------------------------------

-------------------------------------------------------------

-------------------------------------------------------------

-------------------------------------------------------------

5. Consider the diverse perspectives that different individuals can bring to your goals. How can you actively seek out and incorporate diverse viewpoints into your decision-making process?

-------------------------------------------------------------

-------------------------------------------------------------

-------------------------------------------------------------

-------------------------------------------------------------

-------------------------------------------------------------

-------------------------------------------------------------

6. How do you envision your support network evolving as you work towards your long-term goals? What steps can you take to strengthen and expand this network?

-------------------------------------------------------------

-------------------------------------------------------------

-------------------------------------------------------------

-------------------------------------------------------------

---------------------------------------------------------------

---------------------------------------------------------------

7. Reflect on a time when you hesitated to ask for help due to fear or insecurity. What strategies can you employ to overcome such hesitations in the future?

---------------------------------------------------------------

---------------------------------------------------------------

---------------------------------------------------------------

---------------------------------------------------------------

---------------------------------------------------------------

---------------------------------------------------------------

8. Consider the role of feedback in the pursuit of your goals. How can you actively seek and utilize constructive feedback from others to refine your approach?

---------------------------------------------------------------

---------------------------------------------------------------

---------------------------------------------------------------

------------------------------------------------

------------------------------------------------

------------------------------------------------

9. Reflect on the balance between independence and collaboration in goal achievement. How can you strike a balance that allows you to leverage the strengths of both approaches?

------------------------------------------------

------------------------------------------------

------------------------------------------------

------------------------------------------------

------------------------------------------------

------------------------------------------------

10. Think about a current goal you are working towards. How might involving others in the pursuit of this goal contribute not only to your success but also to the collective success of your support network?

------------------------------------------------

------------------------------------------------

----------------------------------------------------------

----------------------------------------------------------

----------------------------------------------------------

----------------------------------------------------------

## Take a time-out:

## Key Lessons

1. Understanding the Purpose of Time-Out:
   The chapter emphasizes the importance of taking a time-out as a constructive strategy to manage emotions and behaviors. It serves as a tool to help you regain control and make better decisions.
2. Identifying Triggers and Signs:
   Learn to recognize your triggers and signs that indicate it's time for a time-out. By understanding what leads to challenging behaviors, you can proactively take steps to prevent negative situations.
3. Developing a Personal Time-Out Plan:
   Create a customized time-out plan that suits your needs and preferences. This involves selecting a calm and safe space, setting a specific duration, and deciding on activities that help you relax and reflect.
4. Using Time-Out for Self-Reflection:
   Time-outs are not just about removing yourself from a situation but also about reflecting on your thoughts and actions. Use this time to consider

alternative responses and problem-solving strategies.

5. Communicating Effectively After a Time-Out:

Chapter 8 underscores the importance of communicating openly after a time-out. Learn how to express your feelings, thoughts, and intentions calmly and respectfully, fostering better understanding with others.

## Reflection Questions

1. How can you identify the specific triggers that lead to the need for a time-out in your daily life?

-----------------------------------------------------------

-----------------------------------------------------------

-----------------------------------------------------------

-----------------------------------------------------------

-----------------------------------------------------------

-----------------------------------------------------------

2. In what ways can you personalize your time-out plan to make it more effective for your unique needs and preferences?

-----------------------------------------------------------

-----------------------------------------------------------

----------------------------------------

----------------------------------------

----------------------------------------

----------------------------------------

3. What signs or cues can you pay attention to that signal the ideal time to take a time-out before emotions escalate?

----------------------------------------

----------------------------------------

----------------------------------------

----------------------------------------

----------------------------------------

----------------------------------------

4. How do you envision incorporating self-reflection into your time-out routine to gain insights into your behavior patterns?

----------------------------------------

----------------------------------------

----------------------------------------

---------------------------------------------------------------

---------------------------------------------------------------

---------------------------------------------------------------

5. What strategies can you implement during a time-out to ensure you are using the break productively for self-improvement?

---------------------------------------------------------------

---------------------------------------------------------------

---------------------------------------------------------------

---------------------------------------------------------------

---------------------------------------------------------------

---------------------------------------------------------------

6. In what manner can you communicate your decision to take a time-out to those around you, fostering understanding and cooperation?

---------------------------------------------------------------

---------------------------------------------------------------

---------------------------------------------------------------

---------------------------------------------------------------

----------------------------------------------------------------

----------------------------------------------------------------

7. How will you ensure that the location you choose for your time-out is calm, safe, and conducive to reflection?

----------------------------------------------------------------

----------------------------------------------------------------

----------------------------------------------------------------

----------------------------------------------------------------

----------------------------------------------------------------

8. What activities or practices do you find most helpful in achieving a state of relaxation and composure during a time-out?

----------------------------------------------------------------

----------------------------------------------------------------

----------------------------------------------------------------

----------------------------------------------------------------

----------------------------------------------------------------

-----------------------------------------------------------------

9. How can you maintain consistency in using time-outs as a proactive strategy for behavior management in various situations?

-----------------------------------------------------------------

-----------------------------------------------------------------

-----------------------------------------------------------------

-----------------------------------------------------------------

-----------------------------------------------------------------

-----------------------------------------------------------------

10. What steps will you take to initiate open and respectful communication with others once the time-out period is over, addressing any underlying issues or conflicts
Effectively?

-----------------------------------------------------------------

-----------------------------------------------------------------

-----------------------------------------------------------------

-----------------------------------------------------------------

## Set up a point sheet together:

## Key Lessons

1. Collaborative Goal Setting: In setting up a point sheet together, the chapter emphasizes the importance of involving both parents and children in the process. This collaborative approach fosters a sense of shared responsibility and ensures that the goals set are realistic and achievable.

2. Positive Reinforcement: The chapter underscores the effectiveness of positive reinforcement in shaping behavior. By using a point sheet, parents and children can focus on acknowledging and rewarding positive behaviors, creating a more encouraging and constructive environment.

3. Clear Communication: Establishing open and clear communication is vital in the process of setting up a point sheet. The chapter highlights the need for parents to articulate expectations and guidelines while also allowing children to express their thoughts and concerns, promoting mutual understanding.

4. Consistency is Key: Consistency is identified as a crucial factor in the success of the point sheet strategy. Both parents and children need to adhere

to the agreed-upon rules and consequences consistently, reinforcing the desired behaviors and discouraging negative ones effectively.

5. Adaptability and Flexibility: The chapter stresses the importance of being adaptable to changing circumstances. Life is dynamic, and the point sheet should evolve as children grow and situations change, ensuring that the strategy remains relevant and effective over time.

## Reflection Questions

1. What are your specific goals for setting up a point sheet, and how can you ensure they are realistic and achievable?

------------------------------------------------------------

------------------------------------------------------------

------------------------------------------------------------

------------------------------------------------------------

------------------------------------------------------------

------------------------------------------------------------

2. In what ways can you incorporate positive reinforcement into your daily interactions with your child, fostering a more encouraging environment?

--------------------------------------------------------

--------------------------------------------------------

--------------------------------------------------------

--------------------------------------------------------

--------------------------------------------------------

--------------------------------------------------------

3. How can you improve the clarity of communication with your child when establishing expectations and guidelines for the point sheet?

--------------------------------------------------------

--------------------------------------------------------

--------------------------------------------------------

--------------------------------------------------------

--------------------------------------------------------

--------------------------------------------------------

4. What steps can you take to ensure consistency in applying rules and consequences outlined in the point sheet, both by you and your child?

---------------------------------------------------------

---------------------------------------------------------

---------------------------------------------------------

---------------------------------------------------------

---------------------------------------------------------

---------------------------------------------------------

5. How can you involve your child in the process of adapting the point sheet to changing circumstances, promoting a sense of ownership and responsibility?

---------------------------------------------------------

---------------------------------------------------------

---------------------------------------------------------

---------------------------------------------------------

---------------------------------------------------------

---------------------------------------------------------

6. What positive behaviors do you observe in your child that can be reinforced through the point sheet, and how can you tailor the rewards to their preferences?

--------------------------------------------------------

--------------------------------------------------------

--------------------------------------------------------

--------------------------------------------------------

--------------------------------------------------------

--------------------------------------------------------

7. In what ways can you create a balance between providing structure through the point sheet and allowing your child to express their thoughts and concerns?

--------------------------------------------------------

--------------------------------------------------------

--------------------------------------------------------

--------------------------------------------------------

--------------------------------------------------------

--------------------------------------------------------

8. How can you celebrate the small victories and achievements documented on the point sheet,

reinforcing the motivation for your child to continue making positive choices?

------------------------------------------------------------

------------------------------------------------------------

------------------------------------------------------------

------------------------------------------------------------

------------------------------------------------------------

------------------------------------------------------------

9. What strategies can you implement to remain patient and supportive during the initial phases of using the point sheet, recognizing that behavior change takes time?

------------------------------------------------------------

------------------------------------------------------------

------------------------------------------------------------

------------------------------------------------------------

------------------------------------------------------------

------------------------------------------------------------

10. How can you ensure that the point sheet

remains a dynamic tool that adapts to your child's developmental stages and the evolving nature of family life?

-----------------------------------------------------------

-----------------------------------------------------------

-----------------------------------------------------------

-----------------------------------------------------------

-----------------------------------------------------------

-----------------------------------------------------------

## More ideas for feeling good at home:

## Tell family adults about your good choices:
## Key Lessons

1. Open Communication: One of the primary lessons from this chapter is the importance of open communication with family adults. Sharing your positive choices with them builds trust and strengthens your relationship.
2. Accountability: The chapter emphasizes the concept of accountability. When you willingly share your good choices, you take responsibility for your actions and showcase a sense of maturity.

3. Building Support Systems: Telling family adults about your good choices helps in creating a supportive environment. It allows them to understand your efforts and encourages positive reinforcement.

4. Celebrating Success: This lesson highlights the significance of celebrating your successes. By sharing your achievements with family adults, you create opportunities for acknowledgment and positive reinforcement.

5. Learning from Experiences: The chapter underscores the idea that discussing your good choices with family adults is not just about sharing success but also about learning from the experience. It opens avenues for constructive feedback and personal growth.

## Reflection Questions

1. How do you approach the task of telling family adults about your good choices?

------------------------------------------------------------

------------------------------------------------------------

------------------------------------------------------------

------------------------------------------------------------

------------------------------------------------------------

------------------------------------------------------------

2. What motivates you to share your positive decisions with your family adults?

------------------------------------------------

------------------------------------------------

------------------------------------------------

------------------------------------------------

------------------------------------------------

------------------------------------------------

3. In what ways have you noticed that open communication about your good choices strengthens your relationship with family adults?

------------------------------------------------

------------------------------------------------

------------------------------------------------

------------------------------------------------

------------------------------------------------

------------------------------------------------

4. How do you hold yourself accountable when

communicating about your actions and decisions with your family adults?

------------------------------------------------

------------------------------------------------

------------------------------------------------

------------------------------------------------

------------------------------------------------

------------------------------------------------

5. What strategies do you use to build a support system through sharing your good choices with your family adults?

------------------------------------------------

------------------------------------------------

------------------------------------------------

------------------------------------------------

------------------------------------------------

------------------------------------------------

6. Can you recall a specific instance where telling your family adults about your good choices

resulted in positive reinforcement or acknowledgment?

---------------------------------------------------------------

---------------------------------------------------------------

---------------------------------------------------------------

---------------------------------------------------------------

---------------------------------------------------------------

---------------------------------------------------------------

7. How do you celebrate your successes when sharing them with your family and adults?

---------------------------------------------------------------

---------------------------------------------------------------

---------------------------------------------------------------

---------------------------------------------------------------

---------------------------------------------------------------

---------------------------------------------------------------

8. In what ways has the practice of discussing your good choices with family adults contributed to your personal growth?

-------------------------------------------------

-------------------------------------------------

-------------------------------------------------

-------------------------------------------------

-------------------------------------------------

-------------------------------------------------

9. Do you find that learning from the experiences shared with family adults enhances your decision-making process?

-------------------------------------------------

-------------------------------------------------

-------------------------------------------------

-------------------------------------------------

-------------------------------------------------

-------------------------------------------------

10. How can you integrate the lessons from this chapter into your daily life, making communication about your good choices with family adults a consistent and positive practice?

----------------------------------------------------------

----------------------------------------------------------

----------------------------------------------------------

----------------------------------------------------------

----------------------------------------------------------

----------------------------------------------------------

## Be sure your teachers share the good news

## Key Lessons

1. Recognition and Encouragement Matter: Chapter 9 emphasizes the importance of teachers acknowledging and praising positive behavior. Recognition can significantly impact a student's motivation and self-esteem.
2. Building Positive Relationships: The chapter highlights the role of positive communication in fostering a strong teacher-student relationship. When teachers share the good news, it helps create a supportive and encouraging learning environment.
3. Reinforcement for Good Choices: Teachers play a crucial role in reinforcing positive behaviors. By sharing good news, they contribute to reinforcing

the importance of making good choices and showcase the benefits of positive behavior.

4. Boosting Confidence: Positive feedback and acknowledgment of achievements contribute to boosting a student's confidence. Chapter 9 emphasizes that when teachers share the good news, it positively influences a student's self-perception.

5. Promoting a Positive Classroom Culture: The act of sharing good news contributes to creating a positive classroom culture. This chapter highlights the ripple effect of positivity and how it can impact the overall atmosphere within the classroom.

## Reflection Questions

1. How have you observed your teachers acknowledging positive behavior in the classroom?

------------------------------------------------------------

------------------------------------------------------------

------------------------------------------------------------

------------------------------------------------------------

------------------------------------------------------------

------------------------------------------------------------

2. In what ways do you think the sharing of good news by teachers influences the overall classroom environment?

---------------------------------------------------------

---------------------------------------------------------

---------------------------------------------------------

---------------------------------------------------------

---------------------------------------------------------

---------------------------------------------------------

3. Can you recall a specific instance where a teacher's positive reinforcement impacted your motivation to make good choices?

---------------------------------------------------------

---------------------------------------------------------

---------------------------------------------------------

---------------------------------------------------------

---------------------------------------------------------

---------------------------------------------------------

4. How do you believe positive teacher-student relationships contribute to a healthier learning atmosphere?

-----------------------------------------

-----------------------------------------

-----------------------------------------

-----------------------------------------

-----------------------------------------

-----------------------------------------

5. Reflect on a time when a teacher's recognition made you feel more confident in your abilities.

-----------------------------------------

-----------------------------------------

-----------------------------------------

-----------------------------------------

-----------------------------------------

-----------------------------------------

6. In what ways can teachers balance addressing challenging behaviors while still highlighting and sharing positive achievements?

-----------------------------------------

-----------------------------------------

----------------------------------------

----------------------------------------

----------------------------------------

----------------------------------------

7. How might the act of sharing good news contribute to a sense of community and belonging within the classroom?

----------------------------------------

----------------------------------------

----------------------------------------

----------------------------------------

----------------------------------------

8. Consider the long-term effects of teachers consistently sharing positive news. How might this impact a student's behavior and attitude over time?

----------------------------------------

----------------------------------------

----------------------------------------

---------------------------------------------------------------

---------------------------------------------------------------

---------------------------------------------------------------

9. Reflect on the role of positive reinforcement in shaping your behavior and decision-making.

---------------------------------------------------------------

---------------------------------------------------------------

---------------------------------------------------------------

---------------------------------------------------------------

---------------------------------------------------------------

---------------------------------------------------------------

10. How can you contribute to creating a positive classroom culture by encouraging and recognizing the good choices of your peers?

---------------------------------------------------------------

---------------------------------------------------------------

---------------------------------------------------------------

---------------------------------------------------------------

---------------------------------------------------------------

---------------------------------------------------------------

## Make a plan to solve problems:

## Key Lessons

1. Identifying the Problem:
Understanding the importance of clearly defining the problem at hand is the first step in effective problem-solving. By accurately identifying the issue, you set the foundation for creating a targeted and efficient plan.

2. Breaking down the Problem:
Learning to break down complex problems into smaller, more manageable parts allows for a more systematic and strategic approach. This process helps prevent feeling overwhelmed and enables you to focus on solving each aspect one step at a time.

3. Exploring Possible Solutions:
The chapter emphasizes the value of considering multiple solutions to a problem. Encourage creativity and open-mindedness as you explore various options. Recognize that there may be different ways to approach and resolve the issue.

4. Weighing the Pros and Cons:
Evaluating the potential outcomes and consequences of each solution is crucial. This step involves considering both short-term and long-term effects, helping you make informed decisions that align with your goals and values.

5. Implementing and Adapting the Plan:
Once a plan is established, the chapter stresses the importance of taking action. Implement your chosen solution while remaining open to adjustments. Flexibility and adaptability are key elements in successful problem-solving.

## Reflection Questions

1. Identification:
- What techniques can you employ to identify the specific problem you are facing?

-------------------------------------------------------
-------------------------------------------------------
-------------------------------------------------------
-------------------------------------------------------
-------------------------------------------------------
-------------------------------------------------------

2. Breakdown:

- How can you break down a complex problem into smaller, more manageable parts that you can tackle individually?

-------------------------------------------------------
-------------------------------------------------------

---------------------------------------------------------

---------------------------------------------------------

---------------------------------------------------------

---------------------------------------------------------

## 3. Exploration:

- In what ways can you encourage yourself to think creatively when exploring potential solutions?

---------------------------------------------------------

---------------------------------------------------------

---------------------------------------------------------

---------------------------------------------------------

---------------------------------------------------------

---------------------------------------------------------

## 4. Diversity of Solutions:

- How can you ensure that you consider a variety of solutions before settling on one to address the problem?

---------------------------------------------------------

---------------------------------------------------------

---------------------------------------------------------

-------------------------------------------------------

-------------------------------------------------------

-------------------------------------------------------

## 5. Pros and Cons:

- What methods will you use to thoroughly evaluate the pros and cons of each potential solution?

-------------------------------------------------------

-------------------------------------------------------

-------------------------------------------------------

-------------------------------------------------------

-------------------------------------------------------

-------------------------------------------------------

## 6. Decision-Making:

- How will you approach decision-making to ensure that your chosen solution aligns with your values?

-------------------------------------------------------

-------------------------------------------------------

-------------------------------------------------------

-------------------------------------------------------

---------------------------------------------------------

---------------------------------------------------------

## 7. Action Planning:

- What steps will you take to implement your chosen solution effectively?

---------------------------------------------------------

---------------------------------------------------------

---------------------------------------------------------

---------------------------------------------------------

---------------------------------------------------------

---------------------------------------------------------

## 8. Monitoring Progress:

- How will you track and evaluate the progress of your plan once it's in motion?

---------------------------------------------------------

---------------------------------------------------------

---------------------------------------------------------

---------------------------------------------------------

---------------------------------------------------------

---------------------------------------------------------

## 9. Adaptability:

- In what ways can you remain flexible and adaptable throughout the problem-solving process?

---------------------------------------------------------------

---------------------------------------------------------------

---------------------------------------------------------------

---------------------------------------------------------------

---------------------------------------------------------------

---------------------------------------------------------------

10. Learning from Experience:

- Reflecting on past problem-solving experiences, how can you apply lessons learned to enhance your future approach to making plans?

---------------------------------------------------------------

---------------------------------------------------------------

---------------------------------------------------------------

---------------------------------------------------------------

---------------------------------------------------------------

---------------------------------------------------------------

## Do kind things for no reason:

## Key Lessons

1. Cultivate Empathy and Compassion:

In the journey of life, practicing kindness without expecting anything in return is a powerful way to nurture empathy and compassion. By embracing this virtue, you contribute positively to the well-being of others and create a more harmonious environment.

2. Foster a Positive Ripple Effect:

Small acts of kindness have the potential to create a ripple effect, influencing others to engage in similar benevolent actions. By doing kind things for no reason, you become a catalyst for positive change, inspiring those around you to spread kindness in their own ways.

3. Build Lasting Connections:

Kindness forms the foundation of meaningful relationships. By engaging in selfless acts, you not only strengthen existing connections but also create opportunities to forge new, genuine bonds. These connections contribute significantly to your overall well-being and support network.

4. Enhance Emotional Well-being:

The act of doing kind things for no reason can have a profound impact on your emotional well-being. It promotes a sense of fulfillment, joy, and satisfaction. Engaging in acts of kindness becomes a source of personal happiness and contributes to a positive mindset.

5. Develop a Positive Self-Image:

Consistently practicing kindness contributes to the development of a positive self-image. Acts of generosity and compassion shape how you perceive yourself, fostering a sense of pride and confidence in your ability to make a positive impact on the world around you.

## Reflection Questions

1. How have you noticed your interactions with others changing when you intentionally do kind things without expecting anything in return?

------------------------------------------------------------

------------------------------------------------------------

------------------------------------------------------------

------------------------------------------------------------

------------------------------------------------------------

------------------------------------------------------------

2. In what ways do you believe the practice of performing random acts of kindness can contribute to building a more compassionate community?

------------------------------------------------------------

------------------------------------------------------------

------------------------------------------------------------

------------------------------------------------------------

---------------------------------------------------------------

---------------------------------------------------------------

3. Can you share an experience where someone's unexpected kindness had a significant impact on your day or perspective? How did it make you feel?

---------------------------------------------------------------

---------------------------------------------------------------

---------------------------------------------------------------

---------------------------------------------------------------

---------------------------------------------------------------

---------------------------------------------------------------

4. Reflect on a recent situation where you chose to do something kind for someone without any specific reason. How did that experience influence your mood and outlook?

---------------------------------------------------------------

---------------------------------------------------------------

---------------------------------------------------------------

---------------------------------------------------------

---------------------------------------------------------

---------------------------------------------------------

5. Consider the people in your life who consistently demonstrate kindness without expecting anything in return. What qualities do you admire in them, and how can you incorporate those qualities into your actions?

---------------------------------------------------------

---------------------------------------------------------

---------------------------------------------------------

---------------------------------------------------------

---------------------------------------------------------

---------------------------------------------------------

6. How do you think engaging in random acts of kindness aligns with your values and beliefs?

---------------------------------------------------------

---------------------------------------------------------

---------------------------------------------------------

-----------------------------------------------------------

-----------------------------------------------------------

-----------------------------------------------------------

7. Reflect on a time when you faced a challenging situation, and someone's unexpected kindness made a positive difference. How did that impact your resilience and ability to cope with difficulties?

-----------------------------------------------------------

-----------------------------------------------------------

-----------------------------------------------------------

-----------------------------------------------------------

-----------------------------------------------------------

-----------------------------------------------------------

8. In what ways do you think practicing kindness for no reason contributes to building a more positive and supportive school or community environment?

---------------------------------------------------------

---------------------------------------------------------

---------------------------------------------------------

---------------------------------------------------------

---------------------------------------------------------

---------------------------------------------------------

9. Consider the concept of a "kindness ripple effect." How might your intentional acts of kindness influence those around you to engage in similar positive behaviors?

---------------------------------------------------------

---------------------------------------------------------

---------------------------------------------------------

---------------------------------------------------------

---------------------------------------------------------

---------------------------------------------------------

10. Reflect on the idea that kindness can be a powerful tool for personal growth. How can consistently incorporating acts of kindness into

your daily life contribute to your overall well-being and character development?

------------------------------------------------------------

------------------------------------------------------------

------------------------------------------------------------

------------------------------------------------------------

------------------------------------------------------------

------------------------------------------------------------

## Say Thanks

## Key Lessons

1. The Power of Gratitude:
   In the chapter "Say Thanks," the author emphasizes the importance of expressing gratitude. Learning to say thanks is a powerful tool for building positive relationships and fostering a sense of appreciation for the people around you.
2. Enhancing Social Skills:
   Saying thanks is not just about politeness; it's a key aspect of social skills. The chapter highlights how expressing gratitude contributes to better communication and helps you navigate social situations more effectively.
3. Building a Positive Environment:

The act of saying thanks contributes to creating a positive and supportive environment. By acknowledging the positive actions of others, you not only uplift their spirits but also contribute to a more harmonious and encouraging atmosphere.

4. Cultivating Empathy:

Saying thanks involves recognizing the efforts and kindness of others. This practice encourages the development of empathy, as it requires understanding and appreciating the feelings and intentions of those around you.

5. Personal Growth and Confidence:

The chapter underscores that expressing gratitude is not only about recognizing others but also about personal growth. Learning to say thanks boosts your self-esteem and confidence, fostering a mindset focused on the positive aspects of life.

## Reflection Questions

1. How can you incorporate the habit of saying thanks into your daily interactions to strengthen your relationships?

\------------------------------------------------------------

\------------------------------------------------------------

\------------------------------------------------------------

\------------------------------------------------------------

---------------------------------------------------------------

---------------------------------------------------------------

2. Reflect on a recent situation where someone did something thoughtful for you. How did expressing thanks impact the dynamics of that interaction?

---------------------------------------------------------------

---------------------------------------------------------------

---------------------------------------------------------------

---------------------------------------------------------------

---------------------------------------------------------------

---------------------------------------------------------------

3. Consider the people in your life, both at home and school. How might consistently saying thanks contribute to a more positive and supportive environment for everyone?

---------------------------------------------------------------

---------------------------------------------------------------

---------------------------------------------------------------

---------------------------------------------------------------

---------------------------------------------------------------

---------------------------------------------------------------

4. Think about a challenging situation where expressing gratitude might have diffused tension or improved the overall mood. How can you apply this lesson in similar future circumstances?

---------------------------------------------------------------

---------------------------------------------------------------

---------------------------------------------------------------

---------------------------------------------------------------

---------------------------------------------------------------

---------------------------------------------------------------

5. In what ways can saying thanks be a tool for enhancing your social skills, especially in group settings or when meeting new people?

---------------------------------------------------------------

---------------------------------------------------------------

---------------------------------------------------------------

---------------------------------------------------------------

---------------------------------------------------------------

---------------------------------------------------------------

6. Reflect on the concept of empathy and how saying thanks connects to understanding and appreciating the efforts and intentions of others. How can this awareness positively impact your relationships?

---------------------------------------------------------------

---------------------------------------------------------------

---------------------------------------------------------------

---------------------------------------------------------------

---------------------------------------------------------------

---------------------------------------------------------------

7. Consider the link between expressing gratitude and personal growth. How does recognizing and acknowledging the positive aspects of your life contribute to your overall sense of confidence and well-being?

---------------------------------------------------------------

---------------------------------------------------------------

---------------------------------------------------------------

---------------------------------------------------------------

---------------------------------------------------------------

---------------------------------------------------------------

8. Identify specific actions or behaviors of your peers or family members that you appreciate but may not have acknowledged. How can you make it a habit to express your thanks for these positive contributions?

---------------------------------------------------------------

---------------------------------------------------------------

---------------------------------------------------------------

---------------------------------------------------------------

---------------------------------------------------------------

---------------------------------------------------------------

9. Reflect on the role of gratitude in building a positive community. How can you actively contribute to creating a more harmonious and encouraging environment through the simple act of saying thanks?

---------------------------------------------------

---------------------------------------------------

---------------------------------------------------

---------------------------------------------------

---------------------------------------------------

---------------------------------------------------

10. Think about a person who may not often receive expressions of gratitude. How can you make a deliberate effort to show appreciation for their efforts and kindness?

---------------------------------------------------

---------------------------------------------------

---------------------------------------------------

---------------------------------------------------

---------------------------------------------------

---------------------------------------------------

## Take care of yourself:

## Key Lessons

1. Understanding the Importance of Self-Care:

- Learn why taking care of yourself is essential for overall well-being.

- Recognize the impact of self-care on mental, emotional, and physical health.

2. Identifying Personal Needs:

- Explore your own needs and preferences for self-care.

- Understand that everyone's self-care routine may be unique.

3. Developing Healthy Habits:

- Establish positive habits that contribute to your well-being.

- Explore activities that bring joy, relaxation, and a sense of accomplishment.

4. Setting Boundaries:

- Learn to set healthy boundaries to protect your emotional and physical space.

- Understand the importance of saying 'no' when necessary.

5. Seeking Support:

- Recognize the value of seeking support from friends, family, or professionals.

- Understand that asking for help is a sign of strength, not weakness.

## Reflection Questions

1. How do you prioritize self-care in your daily life, and what activities contribute to your well-being?

------------------------------------------------

------------------------------------------------

------------------------------------------------

------------------------------------------------

------------------------------------------------

------------------------------------------------

2. What are some specific needs you have
identified for your self-care routine?

------------------------------------------------

------------------------------------------------

------------------------------------------------

------------------------------------------------

------------------------------------------------

------------------------------------------------

3. In what ways do positive habits positively
impact your overall health and happiness?

------------------------------------------------

------------------------------------------------

------------------------------------------------

-------------------------------------------------------------

-------------------------------------------------------------

-------------------------------------------------------------

4. How comfortable are you with setting boundaries to protect your personal space and well-being?

-------------------------------------------------------------

-------------------------------------------------------------

-------------------------------------------------------------

-------------------------------------------------------------

-------------------------------------------------------------

-------------------------------------------------------------

5. Can you share an experience where saying 'no' was essential for your self-care, and what did you learn from it?

-------------------------------------------------------------

-------------------------------------------------------------

-------------------------------------------------------------

-------------------------------------------------------------

-----------------------------------------------------------

-----------------------------------------------------------

6. Who are the individuals or resources you can turn to for support when you need it?

-----------------------------------------------------------

-----------------------------------------------------------

-----------------------------------------------------------

-----------------------------------------------------------

-----------------------------------------------------------

7. How do you handle stress, and what strategies do you employ to maintain a sense of balance?

-----------------------------------------------------------

-----------------------------------------------------------

-----------------------------------------------------------

-----------------------------------------------------------

-----------------------------------------------------------

-----------------------------------------------------------

8. What activities or hobbies bring you joy and relaxation, and how often do you engage in them?

------------------------------------------------

------------------------------------------------

------------------------------------------------

------------------------------------------------

------------------------------------------------

9. Reflect on a time when you neglected your self-care. What were the consequences, and what adjustments could you make moving forward?

------------------------------------------------

------------------------------------------------

------------------------------------------------

------------------------------------------------

------------------------------------------------

10. How can you encourage others in your life to

prioritize their self-care, fostering a culture of well-being and support?

---------------------------------------------------------
---------------------------------------------------------
---------------------------------------------------------
---------------------------------------------------------
---------------------------------------------------------
---------------------------------------------------------

## Six Winning Ways to Work toward Positive Change:

## Remember the golden rule: Key Lessons

1. Understanding the Golden Rule: In Chapter 10 of "The Survival Guide for Kids with Behavior Challenges, "Thomas McIntyre emphasizes the importance of remembering the Golden Rule: treating others the way you want to be treated. This fundamental principle forms the basis for positive social interactions and helps create a supportive environment.

2. Empathy and Perspective:
The chapter highlights the role of empathy in applying the Golden Rule. By putting yourself in

others' shoes, you can gain a better understanding of their feelings and experiences. Developing empathy is crucial for building meaningful connections with those around you.

3. Impact on Relationships:

The Golden Rule has a direct impact on the quality of your relationships. Treating others with kindness and respect fosters a positive atmosphere and encourages reciprocity. The chapter explores how adhering to this rule can contribute to healthier and more fulfilling connections with friends, family, and peers.

4. Decision-Making Guideline:

McIntyre discusses how the Golden Rule can serve as a practical guide in decision-making. When faced with choices, considering how your actions may affect others aligns with the core principle of treating everyone with fairness and consideration.

5. Personal Growth and Responsibility:

Chapter 10 emphasizes that embracing the Golden Rule is not just about external interactions but also a pathway to personal growth. Taking responsibility for your actions and striving to be a positive force in your community are key aspects of living by this rule.

## Reflection Questions

1. How can you incorporate the Golden Rule into your daily interactions to create a more positive environment?

------------------------------------------------------------

------------------------------------------------------------

------------------------------------------------------------

------------------------------------------------------------

------------------------------------------------------------

------------------------------------------------------------

2. In what ways have you observed the Golden Rule positively impacting your relationships with others?

------------------------------------------------------------

------------------------------------------------------------

------------------------------------------------------------

------------------------------------------------------------

------------------------------------------------------------

------------------------------------------------------------

3. Reflect on a recent situation where empathy played a crucial role in applying the Golden Rule. What did you learn from that experience?

----------------------------------------------------------

----------------------------------------------------------

----------------------------------------------------------

----------------------------------------------------------

----------------------------------------------------------

----------------------------------------------------------

4. Consider a decision you made recently. How might applying the Golden Rule have influenced your choice, and what outcomes could have resulted?

----------------------------------------------------------

----------------------------------------------------------

----------------------------------------------------------

----------------------------------------------------------

----------------------------------------------------------

----------------------------------------------------------

5. How does treating others the way you want to be treated contribute to a sense of community and belonging?

---------------------------------------------------------

---------------------------------------------------------

---------------------------------------------------------

---------------------------------------------------------

---------------------------------------------------------

---------------------------------------------------------

6. Reflect on a challenging relationship. How might embracing the Golden Rule improve the dynamics and communication in that relationship?

---------------------------------------------------------

---------------------------------------------------------

---------------------------------------------------------

---------------------------------------------------------

---------------------------------------------------------

---------------------------------------------------------

7. In what areas of your life do you find it most challenging to adhere to the Golden Rule, and why?

---------------------------------------------------

---------------------------------------------------

---------------------------------------------------

---------------------------------------------------

---------------------------------------------------

---------------------------------------------------

8. Consider a time when someone treated you exceptionally well. How did that make you feel, and how can you replicate that experience for others?

---------------------------------------------------

---------------------------------------------------

---------------------------------------------------

---------------------------------------------------

---------------------------------------------------

9. Reflect on the role of personal responsibility in living by the Golden Rule. How does taking ownership of your actions contribute to a positive community?

---------------------------------------------------------------

---------------------------------------------------------------

---------------------------------------------------------------

---------------------------------------------------------------

---------------------------------------------------------------

---------------------------------------------------------------

10. How can you spread awareness of the Golden Rule and its positive impact within your school or community?

---------------------------------------------------------------

---------------------------------------------------------------

---------------------------------------------------------------

---------------------------------------------------------------

---------------------------------------------------------------

---------------------------------------------------------------

## Take responsibility for your actions:

## Key Lessons

1. Understanding Consequences:
Taking responsibility involves recognizing the potential outcomes of your actions. Learn to

anticipate consequences, both positive and negative, before making choices.

2. Ownership of Mistakes:

Accepting mistakes as a natural part of life is essential. Taking responsibility means acknowledging when you've made a misstep and actively seeking ways to make amends.

3. Learning and Growth:

View challenges and setbacks as opportunities for personal growth. Taking responsibility for your actions allows you to learn from experiences, fostering resilience and adaptability.

4. Effective Communication:

Expressing yourself responsibly is a vital skill. Learn to communicate openly, honestly, and respectfully when discussing the impact of your actions with others.

5. Empathy and Understanding:

Recognize the impact your actions may have on others. Taking responsibility involves cultivating empathy and understanding the perspectives of those affected by your choices.

## Reflection Questions

1. How do you approach understanding the potential consequences of your actions before making a decision?

-------------------------------------------------------------

-------------------------------------------------------------

---------------------------------------------------

---------------------------------------------------

---------------------------------------------------

---------------------------------------------------

2. Can you recall a specific situation where you had to take responsibility for a mistake? How did you handle it, and what did you learn from the experience?

---------------------------------------------------

---------------------------------------------------

---------------------------------------------------

---------------------------------------------------

---------------------------------------------------

---------------------------------------------------

3. In what ways do you believe taking responsibility for your actions contributes to personal growth and development?

---------------------------------------------------

---------------------------------------------------

---------------------------------------------------------

---------------------------------------------------------

---------------------------------------------------------

---------------------------------------------------------

4. Reflect on a recent challenge or setback. How did you respond, and what steps did you take to learn from the experience?

---------------------------------------------------------

---------------------------------------------------------

---------------------------------------------------------

---------------------------------------------------------

---------------------------------------------------------

---------------------------------------------------------

5. Consider a time when effective communication played a role in taking responsibility. How did you express yourself responsibly, and what impact did it have on the situation?

---------------------------------------------------------

---------------------------------------------------------

---------------------------------------------------------------

---------------------------------------------------------------

---------------------------------------------------------------

---------------------------------------------------------------

6. How do you balance the need to take responsibility for your actions with the importance of self-forgiveness and moving forward?

---------------------------------------------------------------

---------------------------------------------------------------

---------------------------------------------------------------

---------------------------------------------------------------

---------------------------------------------------------------

---------------------------------------------------------------

7. Reflect on a situation where you had to consider the feelings and perspectives of others while taking responsibility. How did empathy influence your response?

---------------------------------------------------------------

---------------------------------------------------------------

------------------------------------------------

------------------------------------------------

------------------------------------------------

------------------------------------------------

8. Share an example of a positive outcome that resulted from taking responsibility for your actions. What did you do differently in that situation?

------------------------------------------------

------------------------------------------------

------------------------------------------------

------------------------------------------------

------------------------------------------------

------------------------------------------------

9. How do you differentiate between situations where you have control over the outcome and those where external factors play a significant role in the result?

----------------------------------------

----------------------------------------

----------------------------------------

----------------------------------------

----------------------------------------

----------------------------------------

10. Consider the role of responsibility in building and maintaining positive relationships. How does taking responsibility contribute to trust and mutual respect in your interactions with others?

----------------------------------------

----------------------------------------

----------------------------------------

----------------------------------------

----------------------------------------

----------------------------------------

## Be Patient and Persistent
## Key Lessons

1. The Power of Patience:

Patience is a virtue that can significantly impact your journey in overcoming behavior challenges. Understand that change takes time, and practicing patience will help you navigate the ups and downs more effectively.

2. Consistency is Key:

Persistence is your greatest ally when facing behavior challenges. Consistent efforts, even in the face of setbacks, contribute to long-term success. Remember, small, steady steps lead to significant progress.

3. Self-Reflection Fuels Growth:

Take the time to reflect on your actions and behaviors regularly. It's through this self-awareness that you can identify areas for improvement and develop strategies to overcome challenges.

4. Learn from Setbacks:

Setbacks are a natural part of any journey. Instead of letting they discourage you, view setbacks as opportunities to learn and grow. Analyze what went wrong, adjust your approach, and move forward with renewed determination.

5. Celebrate Small Wins:

Acknowledge and celebrate the small victories along the way. Recognizing your progress, no matter how minor boosts your confidence and reinforces the positive changes you're making.

## Reflection Questions

1. How have patience and persistence played a role in your journey to overcome behavior challenges?

---------------------------------------------------------------

---------------------------------------------------------------

---------------------------------------------------------------

---------------------------------------------------------------

---------------------------------------------------------------

---------------------------------------------------------------

2. What strategies have you found most effective in cultivating patience in challenging situations?

---------------------------------------------------------------

---------------------------------------------------------------

---------------------------------------------------------------

---------------------------------------------------------------

---------------------------------------------------------------

---------------------------------------------------------------

3. Reflect on a specific instance where persistence led to a positive outcome in your behavior management efforts.

---------------------------------------------------------------

---------------------------------------------------------------

------------------------------------------------

------------------------------------------------

------------------------------------------------

------------------------------------------------

4. In what ways has consistency in your actions contributed to the progress you've made so far?

------------------------------------------------

------------------------------------------------

------------------------------------------------

------------------------------------------------

------------------------------------------------

------------------------------------------------

5. How do you balance being patient with the need for tangible results in your behavior improvement journey?

------------------------------------------------

------------------------------------------------

------------------------------------------------

------------------------------------------------

------------------------------------------------

------------------------------------------------

6. Can you identify patterns in your behavior through regular self-reflection? How has this awareness impacted your actions?

----------------------------------------------------------

----------------------------------------------------------

----------------------------------------------------------

----------------------------------------------------------

----------------------------------------------------------

----------------------------------------------------------

7. Share an experience where a setback taught you valuable lessons. How did you adjust your approach moving forward?

----------------------------------------------------------

----------------------------------------------------------

----------------------------------------------------------

----------------------------------------------------------

----------------------------------------------------------

----------------------------------------------------------

8. What role does a support system play in maintaining patience and persistence? How can you strengthen your support network?

---------------------------------------------

---------------------------------------------

---------------------------------------------

---------------------------------------------

---------------------------------------------

---------------------------------------------

9. How do you celebrate the small wins in your journey, and how does this celebration motivate you to continue making positive choices?

10. Reflect on the concept of delayed gratification. In what ways have you experienced the benefits of delaying immediate rewards for long-term gains in behavior improvement?

---------------------------------------------

---------------------------------------------

---------------------------------------------

---------------------------------------------

---------------------------------------------

---------------------------------------------

## Learn from experience:

## Key Lessons

1. Embrace Mistakes as Learning Opportunities:

In the journey of personal development, mistakes are inevitable. Instead of viewing them negatively, recognize them as valuable learning experiences. Each misstep provides an opportunity for growth and improvement.

2. Reflect on Consequences:

Understanding the consequences of your actions is crucial. Take the time to reflect on how your choices impact not only yourself but also those around you. Consider the short-term and long-term effects of your decisions.

3. Develop a Growth Mindset:

Cultivate a mindset that sees challenges and setbacks as opportunities for improvement. Embrace challenges with a positive attitude, and believe in your capacity to learn and adapt in any situation.

4. Create a Personal Action Plan:

Based on past experiences, identify patterns of behavior that may have led to challenges. Develop a proactive action plan to make positive choices in similar situations in the future. This empowers you to take control of your behavior.

5. Seek Guidance and Feedback:

Don't hesitate to seek advice from trusted individuals in your life. Whether its friends, family, or mentors, obtaining different perspectives can provide valuable insights. Constructive feedback is a powerful tool for personal growth.

## Reflection Questions

1. What specific mistakes have you made recently, and how can you turn them into learning opportunities?

------------------------------------------------------------

------------------------------------------------------------

------------------------------------------------------------

------------------------------------------------------------

------------------------------------------------------------

------------------------------------------------------------

2. Reflect on a recent choice you made. What were the consequences, and how did they affect you and those around you?

------------------------------------------------------------

------------------------------------------------------------

------------------------------------------------------------

------------------------------------------------------------

------------------------------------------------------------

------------------------------------------------------------

3. In what ways can you adopt a growth mindset to overcome challenges and setbacks in your life?

------------------------------------------------------------

------------------------------------------------------------

------------------------------------------------------------

------------------------------------------------------------

------------------------------------------------------------

------------------------------------------------------------

4. Think about a recurring behavior pattern. What steps can you take to break this pattern and make more positive choices?

------------------------------------------------------------

------------------------------------------------------------

------------------------------------------------------------

------------------------------------------------------------

------------------------------------------------------------

------------------------------------------------------------

5. How can you create a personal action plan to

navigate challenging situations based on lessons learned from past experiences?

------------------------------------------------------------

------------------------------------------------------------

------------------------------------------------------------

------------------------------------------------------------

------------------------------------------------------------

------------------------------------------------------------

6. Who are the trusted individuals in your life from whom you can seek guidance and feedback? How can their perspectives contribute to your personal development?

------------------------------------------------------------

------------------------------------------------------------

------------------------------------------------------------

------------------------------------------------------------

------------------------------------------------------------

------------------------------------------------------------

7. Consider a recent accomplishment. How did

your experiences, both positive and negative, contribute to your success?

---------------------------------------------------------------

---------------------------------------------------------------

---------------------------------------------------------------

---------------------------------------------------------------

---------------------------------------------------------------

---------------------------------------------------------------

8. Are there instances when you've avoided seeking help or guidance? How might seeking assistance have led to a better outcome?

---------------------------------------------------------------

---------------------------------------------------------------

---------------------------------------------------------------

---------------------------------------------------------------

---------------------------------------------------------------

---------------------------------------------------------------

9. Reflect on a time when you faced a challenge with a negative attitude. How could adopting a

more positive mindset have influenced the outcome?

------------------------------------------------
------------------------------------------------
------------------------------------------------
------------------------------------------------
------------------------------------------------
------------------------------------------------

10. What steps can you take to actively apply the lessons from your experiences to enhance your decision-making and behavior in the future?

------------------------------------------------
------------------------------------------------
------------------------------------------------
------------------------------------------------
------------------------------------------------
------------------------------------------------

**Think About Your Future**

# Key Lessons

1. Setting Goals: In this chapter, the author emphasizes the importance of setting realistic and achievable goals for your future. Whether it's academic, personal, or career-oriented, having clear goals can provide direction and motivation.

2. Decision-Making Skills: The chapter delves into the significance of developing strong decision-making skills. Learning to evaluate choices, consider consequences, and make informed decisions is crucial for shaping a positive future.

3. Time Management: "Think about Your Future" highlights the value of effective time management. Learning how to prioritize tasks, set deadlines, and allocate time wisely can lead to increased productivity and success in various aspects of life.

4. Building Resilience: The ability to bounce back from setbacks and challenges is a key theme. Resilience is presented as a valuable trait that can help you navigate difficulties and continue working towards your goals despite obstacles.

5. Understanding Consequences: The chapter underscores the importance of recognizing the consequences of your actions. By thinking ahead and considering the impact of your choices, you can avoid potential pitfalls and work towards a future aligned with your aspirations.

## Reflection Questions

1. How do you currently approach setting goals for yourself, and what steps can you take to make your goals more concrete and achievable?

------------------------------------------------------------

------------------------------------------------------------

------------------------------------------------------------

------------------------------------------------------------

------------------------------------------------------------

------------------------------------------------------------

2. Reflect on a recent decision you made. What factors did you consider, and how might your decision-making process be improved for better outcomes in the future?

------------------------------------------------------------

------------------------------------------------------------

------------------------------------------------------------

------------------------------------------------------------

------------------------------------------------------------

------------------------------------------------------------

3. Assess your current time management skills.

Are there areas where you can improve in terms of prioritization and allocating time to different responsibilities?

---------------------------------------------------------------

---------------------------------------------------------------

---------------------------------------------------------------

---------------------------------------------------------------

---------------------------------------------------------------

---------------------------------------------------------------

4. Consider a challenging situation you've faced recently. How did you respond, and what aspects of resilience were evident in your actions? How could you enhance your resilience in similar situations?

---------------------------------------------------------------

---------------------------------------------------------------

---------------------------------------------------------------

---------------------------------------------------------------

---------------------------------------------------------------

---------------------------------------------------------------

5. Think about your long-term aspirations. How do your current actions align with those future goals, and are there any adjustments you need to make?

---------------------------------------------------------------

---------------------------------------------------------------

---------------------------------------------------------------

---------------------------------------------------------------

---------------------------------------------------------------

---------------------------------------------------------------

6. Reflect on a past mistake or misjudgment. What were the consequences, and how can you use this experience to make more informed choices in the future?

---------------------------------------------------------------

---------------------------------------------------------------

---------------------------------------------------------------

---------------------------------------------------------------

---------------------------------------------------------------

---------------------------------------------------------------

7. Consider the role of patience in achieving long-term goals. How can you cultivate patience and perseverance in the face of challenges?

---------------------------------------------------------------

---------------------------------------------------------------

---------------------------------------------------------------

---------------------------------------------------------------

---------------------------------------------------------------

---------------------------------------------------------------

8. Evaluate your current support system. Who are the people in your life who contribute positively to your plans, and how can you strengthen those relationships?

---------------------------------------------------------------

---------------------------------------------------------------

---------------------------------------------------------------

---------------------------------------------------------------

---------------------------------------------------------------

---

9. Reflect on the concept of delayed gratification. In what areas of your life can you practice delaying immediate rewards for greater long-term benefits?

---

---

---

---

---

---

10. Think about the skills and knowledge you need for your future endeavors. What steps can you take now to acquire or enhance those skills, ensuring you're well-prepared for what lies ahead?

---

---

---

---

---

---

## Know that you can meet and beat your challenge:

### Key Lessons

1. Self-Belief is Powerful: Understand that believing in yourself is a crucial aspect of overcoming challenges. Trust in your abilities and know that you have the strength to face and conquer difficulties.
2. Challenges Are Opportunities: Shift your perspective on challenges. Instead of viewing them solely as obstacles, recognize them as opportunities for growth and learning. Every challenge you encounter has the potential to make you stronger and more resilient.
3. Mindset Matters: Cultivate a positive mindset. Your thoughts have a significant impact on your actions and outcomes. Adopting an optimistic mindset can empower you to face challenges with determination and creativity.
4. Learn from Setbacks: Embrace setbacks as part of the journey. Recognize that setbacks are not failures but opportunities to learn. Analyze what went wrong, make adjustments, and use these experiences to improve your approach to future challenges.

5. Seek Support: Don't be afraid to ask for help. Whether it's from friends, family, or mentors, having a support system is crucial when facing challenges. Surround yourself with individuals who believe in your capabilities and can provide guidance and encouragement.

## Reflection Questions

1. How has your belief in yourself influenced your ability to overcome challenges in the past?

------------------------------------------------------------

------------------------------------------------------------

------------------------------------------------------------

------------------------------------------------------------

------------------------------------------------------------

------------------------------------------------------------

2. Can you recall a specific challenge that, in hindsight, turned out to be an opportunity for personal growth?

------------------------------------------------------------

------------------------------------------------------------

------------------------------------------------------------

---------------------------------------------------------

---------------------------------------------------------

---------------------------------------------------------

3. How does maintaining a positive mindset contribute to your resilience when facing challenges?

---------------------------------------------------------

---------------------------------------------------------

---------------------------------------------------------

---------------------------------------------------------

---------------------------------------------------------

---------------------------------------------------------

4. Reflect on a setback you've experienced recently. What did you learn from it, and how can you apply that knowledge moving forward?

---------------------------------------------------------

---------------------------------------------------------

---------------------------------------------------------

---------------------------------------------------------

---------------------------------------------------------------

---------------------------------------------------------------

5. In what ways can you shift your perspective on challenges to view them as opportunities rather than obstacles?

---------------------------------------------------------------

---------------------------------------------------------------

---------------------------------------------------------------

---------------------------------------------------------------

---------------------------------------------------------------

---------------------------------------------------------------

6. Who is part of your support system, and how have they assisted you in facing and overcoming challenges?

---------------------------------------------------------------

---------------------------------------------------------------

---------------------------------------------------------------

---------------------------------------------------------------

---------------------------------------------------------------

---------------------------------------------------------------

7. How do you typically react when confronted with a difficult situation, and are there alternative approaches you could explore?

---------------------------------------------------------------

---------------------------------------------------------------

---------------------------------------------------------------

---------------------------------------------------------------

---------------------------------------------------------------

---------------------------------------------------------------

8. Reflect on a time when you doubted your abilities. What strategies can you employ to boost your self-confidence in similar situations?

---------------------------------------------------------------

---------------------------------------------------------------

---------------------------------------------------------------

---------------------------------------------------------------

---------------------------------------------------------------

---------------------------------------------------------------

9. Consider a long-term goal you have. How can breaking it down into smaller, manageable tasks make it less intimidating and more achievable?

------------------------------------------------------------
------------------------------------------------------------
------------------------------------------------------------
------------------------------------------------------------
------------------------------------------------------------
------------------------------------------------------------

10. What steps can you take to ensure that challenges do not define you, but rather, serve as stepping stones toward personal and academic success?

------------------------------------------------------------
------------------------------------------------------------
------------------------------------------------------------
------------------------------------------------------------
------------------------------------------------------------
------------------------------------------------------------

# What's next?

## Key Lessons

In the concluding chapter of "The Survival Guide for Kids with Behavior Challenges" by Thomas McIntyre, readers are presented with valuable insights that serve as a roadmap for navigating their behavioral challenges. Here are five key lessons derived from the chapter:

1. Reflect on Your Progress:

Take the time to evaluate the progress you've made in implementing the strategies discussed throughout the book. Acknowledge your successes and recognize the areas where improvement is still needed.

2. Embrace Responsibility:

Understand the importance of taking responsibility for your actions. Recognize that your choices have consequences and that you have the power to shape your behavior through mindful decision-making.

3. Continuous Learning:

Life is a journey of continuous learning. The chapter emphasizes the significance of being open to new ideas and strategies for self-improvement. Cultivate a mindset that embraces growth and change.

4. Build Supportive Relationships:

Surround yourself with individuals who uplift and support you. Establishing positive connections with family, friends, and mentors can contribute significantly to your emotional well-being and personal development.

5. Set Realistic Goals:

Learn the art of setting realistic and achievable goals. Break down larger objectives into manageable steps, and celebrate your accomplishments along the way. This approach fosters a sense of accomplishment and motivation.

## Reflection Questions

1. How have you seen yourself grow and change since implementing the strategies discussed in the book?

------------------------------------------------------------

------------------------------------------------------------

------------------------------------------------------------

------------------------------------------------------------

------------------------------------------------------------

------------------------------------------------------------

2. In what ways can you take greater responsibility for your actions and the impact they have on those around you?

----------------------------------------------------------

----------------------------------------------------------

----------------------------------------------------------

----------------------------------------------------------

----------------------------------------------------------

----------------------------------------------------------

3. What new ideas or strategies have you discovered in this chapter that you are willing to incorporate into your daily life?

----------------------------------------------------------

----------------------------------------------------------

----------------------------------------------------------

----------------------------------------------------------

----------------------------------------------------------

----------------------------------------------------------

4. Who are the supportive individuals in your life, and how can you strengthen those relationships for continued growth?

---------------------------------------------------------

---------------------------------------------------------

---------------------------------------------------------

---------------------------------------------------------

---------------------------------------------------------

---------------------------------------------------------

5. Reflect on a specific behavioral goal you've set for yourself. What steps can you take to break it down into smaller, achievable tasks?

---------------------------------------------------------

---------------------------------------------------------

---------------------------------------------------------

---------------------------------------------------------

---------------------------------------------------------

---------------------------------------------------------

6. How do you handle setbacks or challenges, and what adjustments can you make to overcome them in the future?

-----------------------------------------------------------

-----------------------------------------------------------

-----------------------------------------------------------

-----------------------------------------------------------

-----------------------------------------------------------

-----------------------------------------------------------

7. In what areas do you feel you still need to learn and grow, and what resources or support can assist you in that process?

-----------------------------------------------------------

-----------------------------------------------------------

-----------------------------------------------------------

-----------------------------------------------------------

-----------------------------------------------------------

-----------------------------------------------------------

8. Consider the impact of your choices on your relationships. How can you ensure that your decisions positively contribute to your connections with others?

---------------------------------------------------------

---------------------------------------------------------

---------------------------------------------------------

---------------------------------------------------------

---------------------------------------------------------

---------------------------------------------------------

9. What are some realistic short-term and long-term goals you can set for yourself to continue progressing on your behavioral journey?

---------------------------------------------------------

---------------------------------------------------------

---------------------------------------------------------

---------------------------------------------------------

---------------------------------------------------------

---------------------------------------------------------

10. How can you celebrate your achievements, both big and small, to maintain motivation and a positive outlook on your behavioral challenges?

----------------------------------------

----------------------------------------

----------------------------------------

----------------------------------------

----------------------------------------

----------------------------------------

## What is BD? What does BD mean?

## Key Lessons

1. Definition of BD (Behavioral Disorders):
   Understanding what BD means is crucial for fostering empathy and support for individuals facing behavioral challenges. BD encompasses a range of behavioral disorders that may impact a person's ability to make good choices and navigate social situations.

2. Recognizing Signs and Symptoms:
   Learn to identify signs and symptoms associated with BD. This includes understanding behavioral patterns, emotional triggers, and the impact of environmental factors on an individual's behavior. Recognition is the first step towards effective intervention and support.

3. Empathy and Compassion:

Cultivate empathy and compassion for those dealing with BD. Recognize that behavior challenges are often linked to underlying difficulties, and approaching individuals with understanding can create a more supportive environment.

4. Effective Communication Strategies:

Explore effective communication strategies when interacting with someone with BD. Clear and respectful communication can enhance understanding and cooperation, fostering a positive relationship between individuals with behavioral challenges and their peers.

5. Promoting a Positive Environment:

Create and maintain a positive and inclusive environment for everyone, including those with BD. Emphasize the importance of teamwork, kindness, and acceptance to promote a sense of belonging and reduce the likelihood of behavioral challenges.

## Reflection Questions

1. What are the key characteristics of BD, and how can recognizing these traits contribute to a more supportive community for individuals facing behavioral challenges?

-------------------------------------------------------------

-------------------------------------------------------------

-------------------------------------------------------------

---------------------------------------------------

---------------------------------------------------

---------------------------------------------------

2. How can you demonstrate empathy and compassion towards someone with BD in your daily interactions? Share specific examples.

---------------------------------------------------

---------------------------------------------------

---------------------------------------------------

---------------------------------------------------

---------------------------------------------------

---------------------------------------------------

3. Reflect on instances when effective communication strategies were employed in dealing with behavior challenges. What positive outcomes resulted from these strategies?

---------------------------------------------------

---------------------------------------------------

---------------------------------------------------

------------------------------------------------------------

------------------------------------------------------------

------------------------------------------------------------

4. In what ways can you contribute to creating a positive and inclusive environment that fosters understanding and acceptance for individuals with BD?

------------------------------------------------------------

------------------------------------------------------------

------------------------------------------------------------

------------------------------------------------------------

------------------------------------------------------------

------------------------------------------------------------

5. Consider the impact of environmental factors on behavior. How can you help modify or adapt the environment to better support individuals with BD?

------------------------------------------------------------

------------------------------------------------------------

---------------------------------------------------

---------------------------------------------------

---------------------------------------------------

---------------------------------------------------

6. What role does education play in reducing stigma associated with BD, and how can you actively contribute to promoting awareness and understanding?

---------------------------------------------------

---------------------------------------------------

---------------------------------------------------

---------------------------------------------------

---------------------------------------------------

---------------------------------------------------

7. Reflect on a time when you witnessed someone demonstrating resilience in the face of behavior challenges. What qualities did they exhibit, and what can you learn from their experience?

------------------------------------------------------------

------------------------------------------------------------

------------------------------------------------------------

------------------------------------------------------------

------------------------------------------------------------

------------------------------------------------------------

8. How does a supportive community positively influence the well-being of individuals with BD? What actions can you take to contribute to such a community?

------------------------------------------------------------

------------------------------------------------------------

------------------------------------------------------------

------------------------------------------------------------

------------------------------------------------------------

------------------------------------------------------------

9. Think about the importance of setting boundaries when interacting with individuals facing behavioral challenges. How can clear

boundaries be established without compromising empathy?

------------------------------------------------

------------------------------------------------

------------------------------------------------

------------------------------------------------

------------------------------------------------

10. Reflect on the role of patience in building relationships with individuals with BD. How can you cultivate patience in your interactions and reactions to behavior challenges?

------------------------------------------------

------------------------------------------------

------------------------------------------------

------------------------------------------------

------------------------------------------------

------------------------------------------------

## What BD does not mean:

# Key Lessons

1. Behavior Disorder (BD) is not synonymous with a flawed character:
Understanding that having a behavior disorder does not make a person inherently bad or flawed is crucial. It is a condition that can be managed and improved with the right strategies and support.

2. BD does not define your potential:
Individuals with behavior disorders should recognize that their diagnosis does not determine their capabilities or limit their potential. With the right interventions, they can achieve success and lead fulfilling lives.

3. BD is not an excuse for irresponsible behavior:
Acknowledging the disorder does not give anyone a free pass for irresponsible actions. It's essential to take responsibility for one's behavior and work towards making positive choices despite the challenges associated with BD.

4. BD does not exempt you from consequences:
While understanding the challenges associated with behavior disorders, individuals must recognize that consequences are a part of life. BD does not excuse one from facing the outcomes of their actions, and learning from these consequences is integral to personal growth.

5. BD does not mean isolation:
Individuals with behavior disorders should actively seek and cultivate positive relationships. Isolation is not a solution; instead, building connections

with understanding individuals and seeking support networks can contribute to personal growth and development.

## Reflection Questions

1. How can you differentiate between someone's behavior and their character traits when dealing with individuals with behavior disorders?

--------------------------------------------------------

--------------------------------------------------------

--------------------------------------------------------

--------------------------------------------------------

--------------------------------------------------------

--------------------------------------------------------

2. In what ways can individuals with behavior disorders overcome societal stereotypes and showcase their true potential?

--------------------------------------------------------

--------------------------------------------------------

--------------------------------------------------------

--------------------------------------------------------

---------------------------------------------------------

---------------------------------------------------------

3. How do you think acknowledging the challenges associated with BD can empower individuals to take control of their actions?

---------------------------------------------------------

---------------------------------------------------------

---------------------------------------------------------

---------------------------------------------------------

---------------------------------------------------------

---------------------------------------------------------

4. Reflect on a situation where someone with BD took responsibility for their actions. What positive outcomes resulted from this accountability?

---------------------------------------------------------

---------------------------------------------------------

---------------------------------------------------------

---------------------------------------------------------

---------------------------------------------------------

-----------------------------------------------------------------

5. How can the understanding that consequences are a part of life positively impact decision-making for individuals with behavior disorders?

-----------------------------------------------------------------

-----------------------------------------------------------------

-----------------------------------------------------------------

-----------------------------------------------------------------

-----------------------------------------------------------------

-----------------------------------------------------------------

6. What strategies can individuals with behavior disorders employ to build and maintain positive relationships despite the challenges they may face?

-----------------------------------------------------------------

-----------------------------------------------------------------

-----------------------------------------------------------------

-----------------------------------------------------------------

-----------------------------------------------------------------

-----------------------------------------------------------------

7. Reflect on a time when you witnessed someone with BD overcoming obstacles to achieve success. What lessons can be drawn from that experience?

------------------------------------------------------------

------------------------------------------------------------

------------------------------------------------------------

------------------------------------------------------------

------------------------------------------------------------

------------------------------------------------------------

8. In what ways can society support individuals with behavior disorders to ensure they are not marginalized or isolated?

------------------------------------------------------------

------------------------------------------------------------

------------------------------------------------------------

------------------------------------------------------------

------------------------------------------------------------

------------------------------------------------------------

9. How can fostering a sense of community and

empathy contribute to the overall well-being of individuals with behavior disorders?

---------------------------------------------------------

---------------------------------------------------------

---------------------------------------------------------

---------------------------------------------------------

---------------------------------------------------------

---------------------------------------------------------

10. What role does self-advocacy play in challenging stereotypes associated with BD, and how can individuals with behavior disorders become advocates for themselves and others?

---------------------------------------------------------

---------------------------------------------------------

---------------------------------------------------------

---------------------------------------------------------

---------------------------------------------------------

---------------------------------------------------------

## It's tough to be a kid with BD:

# Key Lessons

1. Understanding Behavior Challenges: The chapter emphasizes the challenges that kids with Behavioral Disorders (BD) face and aims to foster a deeper understanding of their struggles.

2. Empathy and Patience: Developing empathy and patience is crucial when interacting with individuals dealing with BD. The chapter discusses the importance of recognizing the unique needs and experiences of these children.

3. Building a Support System: Creating a strong support system is vital for kids with BD. The book explores the significance of having a network that includes family, friends, and educators to help navigate the challenges effectively.

4. Self-Advocacy: Teaching children with BD to advocate for themselves is a key focus. The chapter provides strategies for kids to express their needs and emotions constructively, fostering independence and resilience.

5. Positive Choices and Consequences: The chapter highlights the connection between making positive choices and experiencing favorable consequences. It delves into the importance of teaching kids with BD about cause and effect to promote responsible decision-making.

## Reflection Questions

1. How can you deepen your understanding of the challenges faced by kids with BD to enhance your interactions with them?

---------------------------------------------------------------

---------------------------------------------------------------

---------------------------------------------------------------

---------------------------------------------------------------

---------------------------------------------------------------

---------------------------------------------------------------

2. In what ways can you demonstrate empathy and patience when dealing with a child who has Behavioral Disorders?

---------------------------------------------------------------

---------------------------------------------------------------

---------------------------------------------------------------

---------------------------------------------------------------

---------------------------------------------------------------

---------------------------------------------------------------

3. Reflect on your current support system. How

can you strengthen it to better assist a child with BD in your life?

-----------------------------------------------------------

-----------------------------------------------------------

-----------------------------------------------------------

-----------------------------------------------------------

-----------------------------------------------------------

-----------------------------------------------------------

4. How can you actively contribute to creating a more inclusive and supportive environment for children with BD, both at home and in educational settings?

-----------------------------------------------------------

-----------------------------------------------------------

-----------------------------------------------------------

-----------------------------------------------------------

-----------------------------------------------------------

-----------------------------------------------------------

5. What strategies can you implement to help a

child with BD become more self-advocating and expressive of their needs?

------------------------------------------------------------

------------------------------------------------------------

------------------------------------------------------------

------------------------------------------------------------

------------------------------------------------------------

------------------------------------------------------------

6. Consider the positive choices you've witnessed in children with BD. How can you reinforce and encourage these behaviors?

------------------------------------------------------------

------------------------------------------------------------

------------------------------------------------------------

------------------------------------------------------------

------------------------------------------------------------

------------------------------------------------------------

7. Reflect on the consequences, both positive and negative, that children with BD may face. How can

you help them understand and navigate these outcomes?

---------------------------------------------------------

---------------------------------------------------------

---------------------------------------------------------

---------------------------------------------------------

---------------------------------------------------------

---------------------------------------------------------

8. How can you involve the child with BD in decision-making processes, fostering a sense of autonomy and responsibility?

---------------------------------------------------------

---------------------------------------------------------

---------------------------------------------------------

---------------------------------------------------------

---------------------------------------------------------

---------------------------------------------------------

9. Reflect on instances where patience has played a

crucial role in your interactions with a child with BD. How can you further cultivate this virtue?

-------------------------------------------------------

-------------------------------------------------------

-------------------------------------------------------

-------------------------------------------------------

-------------------------------------------------------

-------------------------------------------------------

10. In what ways can you contribute to promoting a positive and understanding community for kids with BD, fostering an environment where they feel accepted and valued?

-------------------------------------------------------

-------------------------------------------------------

-------------------------------------------------------

-------------------------------------------------------

-------------------------------------------------------

-------------------------------------------------------

## Don't use BD as an Excuse:
## Key Lessons

1. Taking Responsibility:
   In this chapter, the author emphasizes the importance of taking responsibility for one's actions. Rather than using Behavioral Disorders (BD) as an excuse, it encourages individuals to acknowledge their behaviors and work towards positive change.
2. Empowerment through Accountability:
   The lesson underscores the idea that by holding oneself accountable, individuals with behavior challenges can empower themselves to make positive choices. This proactive approach allows for personal growth and development.
3. Overcoming Challenges:
   The chapter explores strategies for overcoming challenges associated with BD. It highlights the resilience and strength that individuals can tap into, reminding readers that they are capable of navigating difficulties and making better decisions.
4. Building a Support System:
   A crucial takeaway is the importance of building a supportive network. The chapter explores the role of friends, family, and professionals in assisting individuals with behavior challenges. It stresses the significance of seeking help when needed.
5. Focusing on Solutions:

Rather than dwelling on problems, the chapter encourages a shift in focus toward finding solutions. By adopting a problem-solving mindset, individuals can actively work towards minimizing the impact of BD on their lives and relationships.

## Reflection Questions

1. How have you personally taken responsibility for your actions in the past, especially when facing challenges related to Behavioral Disorders?

------------------------------------------------------------

------------------------------------------------------------

------------------------------------------------------------

------------------------------------------------------------

------------------------------------------------------------

------------------------------------------------------------

2. In what ways do you believe holding yourself accountable can contribute to your personal growth and development?

------------------------------------------------------------

------------------------------------------------------------

------------------------------------------------------------

------------------------------------------------------------

-------------------------------------------------------------

-------------------------------------------------------------

3. Reflect on a specific challenge you've faced recently. How did you overcome it, and what role did taking responsibility play in the process?

-------------------------------------------------------------

-------------------------------------------------------------

-------------------------------------------------------------

-------------------------------------------------------------

-------------------------------------------------------------

-------------------------------------------------------------

4. Who are the key individuals in your support system, and how have they assisted you in navigating challenges associated with BD?

-------------------------------------------------------------

-------------------------------------------------------------

-------------------------------------------------------------

-------------------------------------------------------------

-------------------------------------------------------------

----------------------------------------------------------------

5. Share an instance where you focused on finding a solution rather than dwelling on the problem. What was the outcome, and what did you learn from that experience?

----------------------------------------------------------------

----------------------------------------------------------------

----------------------------------------------------------------

----------------------------------------------------------------

----------------------------------------------------------------

----------------------------------------------------------------

6. How can you actively empower yourself to make positive choices, even in situations where BD might be a factor?

----------------------------------------------------------------

----------------------------------------------------------------

----------------------------------------------------------------

----------------------------------------------------------------

----------------------------------------------------------------

-------------------------------------------------------------

7. Consider the importance of seeking help when needed. What barriers, if any, have you faced in reaching out to friends, family, or professionals for support?

-------------------------------------------------------------

-------------------------------------------------------------

-------------------------------------------------------------

-------------------------------------------------------------

-------------------------------------------------------------

-------------------------------------------------------------

8. Reflect on the role of personal resilience in overcoming challenges related to BD. In what ways have you demonstrated resilience in the face of adversity?

-------------------------------------------------------------

-------------------------------------------------------------

-------------------------------------------------------------

-------------------------------------------------------------

---------------------------------------------------------

---------------------------------------------------------

9. Explore how your mindset towards challenges has evolved. Have you noticed any shifts in your approach to problem-solving?

---------------------------------------------------------

---------------------------------------------------------

---------------------------------------------------------

---------------------------------------------------------

---------------------------------------------------------

---------------------------------------------------------

10. Identify specific actions you can take to minimize the impact of BD on your life and relationships, focusing on proactive and solution-oriented strategies.

---------------------------------------------

---------------------------------------------

---------------------------------------------

---------------------------------------------

---------------------------------------------

---------------------------------------------

## Key Lessons

1. Understanding Consequences
One of the key lessons from Chapter 12 of "The Survival Guide for Kids with Behavior Challenges" is the importance of understanding consequences. Kids need to recognize that every choice they make has an impact, and being aware of potential outcomes helps them make more informed decisions.

2. Developing Empathy
The chapter emphasizes the significance of developing empathy. Learning to consider how their choices may affect others helps kids cultivate empathy, fostering positive relationships and a sense of responsibility for their actions.

3. Building Decision-Making Skills
Kids are guided in the book on how to build effective decision-making skills. By learning to weigh options, consider consequences, and make

thoughtful choices, they empower themselves to navigate challenges more successfully.

4. Setting Personal Boundaries

Another crucial lesson involves setting personal boundaries. Kids are encouraged to identify their limits and communicate them assertively, fostering self-respect and helping them make choices aligned with their values.

5. Seeking Guidance

The importance of seeking guidance is highlighted in Chapter 12. Kids are encouraged to reach out to trusted adults for advice and support, recognizing that seeking help is a sign of strength and wisdom.

## Reflection Questions

1. How do your choices impact those around you, and what can you do to make choices that contribute positively to your relationships?

------------------------------------------------------------

------------------------------------------------------------

------------------------------------------------------------

------------------------------------------------------------

------------------------------------------------------------

------------------------------------------------------------

2. Reflect on a recent decision you made. Were

you aware of the potential consequences, and how did they unfold?

-----------------------------------------------------------

-----------------------------------------------------------

-----------------------------------------------------------

-----------------------------------------------------------

-----------------------------------------------------------

-----------------------------------------------------------

3. How can you actively practice empathy in your daily interactions to better understand the perspectives and feelings of others?

-----------------------------------------------------------

-----------------------------------------------------------

-----------------------------------------------------------

-----------------------------------------------------------

-----------------------------------------------------------

-----------------------------------------------------------

4. What steps can you take to improve your decision-making skills? Consider seeking advice

from a trusted adult or using a decision-making framework.

---

---

---

---

---

---

5. Reflect on a time when you set a personal boundary. How did it contribute to a positive outcome, and how can you establish and communicate boundaries more effectively?

---

---

---

---

---

---

6. Think about a challenging situation you're

currently facing. How can seeking guidance from a trusted adult help you navigate through it?

------------------------------------------------------------

------------------------------------------------------------

------------------------------------------------------------

------------------------------------------------------------

------------------------------------------------------------

------------------------------------------------------------

7. Consider the values that are important to you. How can you ensure that your choices align with these values?

------------------------------------------------------------

------------------------------------------------------------

------------------------------------------------------------

------------------------------------------------------------

------------------------------------------------------------

------------------------------------------------------------

8. Reflect on a past mistake. What did you learn

from it, and how can that knowledge guide you in making better choices in the future?

\------------------------------------------------------------

\------------------------------------------------------------

\------------------------------------------------------------

\------------------------------------------------------------

\------------------------------------------------------------

\------------------------------------------------------------

9. How can you cultivate a mindset of responsibility for your actions, recognizing the power you have to shape your own experiences?

\------------------------------------------------------------

\------------------------------------------------------------

\------------------------------------------------------------

\------------------------------------------------------------

\------------------------------------------------------------

\------------------------------------------------------------

10. In what ways can you teach and share these

lessons with your peers, creating a positive influence on the choices they make?

------------------------------------------------------------

------------------------------------------------------------

------------------------------------------------------------

------------------------------------------------------------

------------------------------------------------------------

------------------------------------------------------------

## Kids whose brain chemicals are mixed up:

### Key Lessons

1. Understanding Neurotransmitters: The chapter sheds light on the role of neurotransmitters in the brain and how imbalances can affect behavior. Learn about the impact of chemicals like dopamine, serotonin, and norepinephrine on mood and decision-making.
2. Recognizing Brain-Based Challenges: Gain insights into identifying and understanding brain-based challenges that some kids face. Recognize that certain behaviors may be linked to neurological factors rather than deliberate choices.
3. Empathy and Compassion: Develop empathy and compassion towards kids with brain chemical imbalances. Recognize that their struggles are

genuine, and a supportive approach can make a significant difference in their lives.

4. Navigating Treatment Options: Explore different treatment options available for kids with brain chemical imbalances. Learn about therapies, medications, and lifestyle adjustments that can help manage symptoms and enhance overall well-being.

5. Building a Supportive Environment: Discover the importance of creating a supportive environment at home, school, and in the community. Understand how a positive and understanding atmosphere can contribute to the well-being of kids facing these challenges.

## Reflection Questions

1. How might the understanding of neurotransmitters enhance your empathy towards kids facing brain chemical imbalances?

-----------------------------------------------------------

-----------------------------------------------------------

-----------------------------------------------------------

-----------------------------------------------------------

-----------------------------------------------------------

-----------------------------------------------------------

2. In what ways can recognizing brain-based

challenges in others impact your interactions and relationships?

------------------------------------------------

------------------------------------------------

------------------------------------------------

------------------------------------------------

------------------------------------------------

------------------------------------------------

3. Reflect on a specific situation where a child's behavior was misunderstood due to a lack of awareness about brain chemical imbalances. How could this understanding have changed the outcome?

------------------------------------------------

------------------------------------------------

------------------------------------------------

------------------------------------------------

------------------------------------------------

------------------------------------------------

4. How can you contribute to creating an inclusive and supportive environment for kids with brain chemical imbalances in your school or community?

---------------------------------------------------------------

---------------------------------------------------------------

---------------------------------------------------------------

---------------------------------------------------------------

---------------------------------------------------------------

---------------------------------------------------------------

5. Consider the treatment options discussed in the chapter. How might these interventions positively influence the lives of kids with neurological challenges?

---------------------------------------------------------------

---------------------------------------------------------------

---------------------------------------------------------------

---------------------------------------------------------------

---------------------------------------------------------------

----------------------------------------------------------------

6. Reflect on the role of empathy in your interactions with peers. How might a more empathetic approach benefit both you and your friends?

----------------------------------------------------------------

----------------------------------------------------------------

----------------------------------------------------------------

----------------------------------------------------------------

----------------------------------------------------------------

----------------------------------------------------------------

7. How can you educate others about the challenges faced by kids with brain chemical imbalances, promoting a more understanding and accepting community?

----------------------------------------------------------------

----------------------------------------------------------------

----------------------------------------------------------------

----------------------------------------------------------------

---------------------------------------------------------

---------------------------------------------------------

8. Explore ways in which teachers and parents can collaborate to support a child with brain-based challenges in both academic and social settings.

---------------------------------------------------------

---------------------------------------------------------

---------------------------------------------------------

---------------------------------------------------------

---------------------------------------------------------

---------------------------------------------------------

9. Reflect on the concept of neurodiversity. How can embracing neurodiversity contribute to a more inclusive and tolerant society?

---------------------------------------------------------

---------------------------------------------------------

---------------------------------------------------------

---------------------------------------------------------

---------------------------------------------------------

10. Consider the long-term impact of a supportive environment on the overall well-being of kids facing brain chemical imbalances. How can you actively contribute to fostering such an environment?

------------------------------------------------------------

------------------------------------------------------------

------------------------------------------------------------

------------------------------------------------------------

------------------------------------------------------------

------------------------------------------------------------

## Kids who learn in different ways:

## Key Lessons

1. Understanding Diverse Learning Styles:
Recognize that children have unique learning styles, and it's essential to embrace and understand these differences to create an inclusive and supportive learning environment.
2. Tailoring Teaching Methods:
Adapt teaching methods to accommodate various learning styles. This flexibility helps ensure that all students, regardless of their preferred learning

approach, can grasp and retain information effectively.

3. Encouraging Peer Collaboration:

Foster an atmosphere of collaboration and teamwork among students with different learning preferences. Encouraging them to work together enhances their understanding and provides an opportunity for shared learning experiences.

4. Promoting Self-Advocacy:

Teach kids to recognize and communicate their preferred learning styles. Encouraging self-advocacy empowers them to seek out the resources and support they need to succeed in their educational journey.

5. Valuing Diversity in Knowledge Acquisition:

Emphasize the importance of recognizing the diverse ways in which individuals acquire knowledge. Promote a culture that values and respects various learning approaches, fostering a sense of appreciation for the richness of diverse perspectives.

## Reflection Questions

1. How would you describe your learning style, and how does it impact your understanding of the material presented in class?

-----------------------------------------------------------------

-----------------------------------------------------------------

-----------------------------------------------------------

-----------------------------------------------------------

-----------------------------------------------------------

-----------------------------------------------------------

2. In what ways have you observed your peers learning differently from you, and how can you leverage these differences for collaborative learning?

-----------------------------------------------------------

-----------------------------------------------------------

-----------------------------------------------------------

-----------------------------------------------------------

-----------------------------------------------------------

-----------------------------------------------------------

3. Reflect on a time when a teacher successfully adapted their teaching method to accommodate different learning styles. How did it positively impact your learning experience?

------------------------------------------------

------------------------------------------------

------------------------------------------------

------------------------------------------------

------------------------------------------------

------------------------------------------------

4. Consider a subject or topic you find challenging. How might recognizing and utilizing your preferred learning style enhance your understanding of that particular subject?

------------------------------------------------

------------------------------------------------

------------------------------------------------

------------------------------------------------

------------------------------------------------

------------------------------------------------

5. How can you contribute to creating a classroom environment that celebrates and values the diversity of learning styles among your classmates?

---------------------------------------------

---------------------------------------------

---------------------------------------------

---------------------------------------------

---------------------------------------------

---------------------------------------------

6. Reflect on a situation where you needed to advocate for yourself in your learning process. What strategies did you use, and what was the outcome?

---------------------------------------------

---------------------------------------------

---------------------------------------------

---------------------------------------------

---------------------------------------------

---------------------------------------------

7. Think about a group project you were involved in. How did the varied learning styles within the

group contribute to the overall success of the project?

---------------------------------------------------------

---------------------------------------------------------

---------------------------------------------------------

---------------------------------------------------------

---------------------------------------------------------

---------------------------------------------------------

8. Consider the role of teachers in fostering a culture of understanding and appreciation for diverse learning styles. What actions can educators take to create an inclusive learning environment?

---------------------------------------------------------

---------------------------------------------------------

---------------------------------------------------------

---------------------------------------------------------

---------------------------------------------------------

---------------------------------------------------------

9. Reflect on a time when you felt misunderstood

or unsupported in your learning journey. What steps could have been taken to better address your unique learning needs?

------------------------------------------------

------------------------------------------------

------------------------------------------------

------------------------------------------------

------------------------------------------------

------------------------------------------------

10. How can the insights gained from understanding diverse learning styles be applied beyond the classroom, in real-world scenarios and future professional endeavors?

------------------------------------------------

------------------------------------------------

------------------------------------------------

------------------------------------------------

------------------------------------------------

------------------------------------------------

## Kids who want attention:

# Key Lessons

1. Understanding the Motivation

In this chapter, Thomas McIntyre delves into the behavior of kids who seek attention. The key lesson here is to understand the underlying motivations driving this behavior. By recognizing the root cause, you can better address and support the child in making positive choices.

2. Positive Attention Alternatives

McIntyre emphasizes the importance of guiding kids toward seeking attention through positive means. By providing alternatives and reinforcing positive behaviors, you can help them develop healthier strategies for gaining attention and recognition.

3. Building Self-Esteem

One of the central themes in this chapter is the impact of self-esteem on attention-seeking behavior. Learn how to foster a positive self-image in kids, as a strong sense of self-worth can reduce the need for external validation through negative attention-seeking behaviors.

4. Setting Clear Boundaries

Establishing clear boundaries is crucial in managing attention-seeking behavior. McIntyre explores effective ways to communicate expectations and consequences, providing a framework that helps kids understand appropriate channels for seeking attention.

5. Collaborating with Teachers and Parents

The chapter highlights the importance of collaboration between educators, parents, and caregivers. By working together, a consistent and supportive approach can be implemented, reinforcing positive behaviors across different environments.

## Reflection Questions

1. How can you identify the specific triggers that lead a child to seek attention inappropriately?

------------------------------------------------------------

------------------------------------------------------------

------------------------------------------------------------

------------------------------------------------------------

------------------------------------------------------------

------------------------------------------------------------

2. In what ways can you encourage positive attention-seeking behaviors in the classroom or at home?

------------------------------------------------------------

------------------------------------------------------------

------------------------------------------------------------

-------------------------------------------------
-------------------------------------------------
-------------------------------------------------

3. How might you contribute to building a child's self-esteem to address attention-seeking tendencies?

-------------------------------------------------
-------------------------------------------------
-------------------------------------------------
-------------------------------------------------
-------------------------------------------------
-------------------------------------------------

4. Reflect on instances where setting clear boundaries has positively impacted a child's behavior. How can you replicate these scenarios?

-------------------------------------------------
-------------------------------------------------
-------------------------------------------------
-------------------------------------------------

---------------------------------------------------------------

---------------------------------------------------------------

5. What strategies can you employ to redirect attention-seeking behaviors toward more positive and constructive outlets?

---------------------------------------------------------------

---------------------------------------------------------------

---------------------------------------------------------------

---------------------------------------------------------------

---------------------------------------------------------------

---------------------------------------------------------------

6. How can you involve parents and caregivers in addressing attention-seeking behaviors to ensure consistency across different environments?

---------------------------------------------------------------

---------------------------------------------------------------

---------------------------------------------------------------

---------------------------------------------------------------

---------------------------------------------------------------

---------------------------------------------------------------

7. Reflect on your communication style. Are your

expectations and consequences communicated to children seeking attention?

--------------------------------------------------------------

--------------------------------------------------------------

--------------------------------------------------------------

--------------------------------------------------------------

--------------------------------------------------------------

--------------------------------------------------------------

8. What role does empathy play in managing attention-seeking behaviors, and how can you cultivate empathy in your interactions with these children?

--------------------------------------------------------------

--------------------------------------------------------------

--------------------------------------------------------------

--------------------------------------------------------------

--------------------------------------------------------------

--------------------------------------------------------------

9. Think about instances where positive reinforcement has been effective. How can you

incorporate more positive reinforcement strategies in your approach?

------------------------------------------------------------

------------------------------------------------------------

------------------------------------------------------------

------------------------------------------------------------

------------------------------------------------------------

------------------------------------------------------------

10. Consider the long-term impact of addressing attention-seeking behaviors. How can your guidance contribute to the child's overall social and emotional development?

------------------------------------------------------------

------------------------------------------------------------

------------------------------------------------------------

------------------------------------------------------------

------------------------------------------------------------

------------------------------------------------------------

# Kids who feel angry and want to get back at someone:

## Key Lessons

1. Understanding Anger: Recognize that feeling angry is a normal emotion, but it is essential to understand and manage it constructively.
2. Negative Consequences: Learn about the potential negative consequences of acting out on anger, such as damaging relationships and getting into trouble.
3. Empathy: Develop empathy by putting yourself in others' shoes, considering their feelings, and understanding the impact of your actions on them.
4. Healthy Communication: Explore effective ways to communicate your feelings without resorting to revenge or harmful behaviors, fostering open and respectful dialogue.
5. Problem Solving: Practice problem-solving skills to address conflicts and challenges constructively, seeking solutions that benefit everyone involved.

## Reflection Questions:

1. How do you typically react when you feel angry, and someone has upset you?

---------------------------------------------

---------------------------------------------

---------------------------------------------

---------------------------------------------

---------------------------------------------

---------------------------------------------

2. Can you recall a time when you acted on your anger impulsively and experienced negative consequences as a result?

---------------------------------------------

---------------------------------------------

---------------------------------------------

---------------------------------------------

---------------------------------------------

---------------------------------------------

3. In what ways can understanding your anger better help you manage it more effectively?

---------------------------------------------

---------------------------------------------

-----------------------------------------------------------
-----------------------------------------------------------
-----------------------------------------------------------
-----------------------------------------------------------

4. Consider a recent situation where you felt angry. How might empathy have influenced your response?

-----------------------------------------------------------
-----------------------------------------------------------
-----------------------------------------------------------
-----------------------------------------------------------
-----------------------------------------------------------
-----------------------------------------------------------

5. How can you differentiate between healthy ways of expressing anger and harmful actions that may lead to regret?

-----------------------------------------------------------
-----------------------------------------------------------
-----------------------------------------------------------

---------------------------------------------------------

---------------------------------------------------------

---------------------------------------------------------

6. Reflect on a time when effective communication diffused a potentially volatile situation. What communication skills were employed?

---------------------------------------------------------

---------------------------------------------------------

---------------------------------------------------------

---------------------------------------------------------

---------------------------------------------------------

---------------------------------------------------------

7. How do you think practicing empathy could improve your relationships with others, even in challenging situations?

---------------------------------------------------------

---------------------------------------------------------

---------------------------------------------------------

---------------------------------------------------------

---------------------------------------------------

---------------------------------------------------

8. What are some alternative ways to express your feelings when angry, besides seeking revenge or getting back at someone?

---------------------------------------------------

---------------------------------------------------

---------------------------------------------------

---------------------------------------------------

---------------------------------------------------

---------------------------------------------------

9. In what ways can problem-solving skills be applied to resolve conflicts without resorting to negative behaviors?

---------------------------------------------------

---------------------------------------------------

---------------------------------------------------

---------------------------------------------------

---------------------------------------------------

---

10. How can you create a support system or seek help from others when you find it challenging to manage your anger on your own?

---

---

---

---

---

---

## Kids who feel bad about themselves:

## Key Lessons

1. Understanding Self-Esteem: In this chapter, Thomas McIntyre explores the concept of self-esteem and how it influences a child's behavior. It emphasizes the importance of recognizing and addressing low self-esteem to foster positive choices.
2. Impact of Negative Labels: The author delves into the detrimental effects of negative labels on children's self-perception. This lesson emphasizes the need to avoid pigeonholing kids and instead

focus on their strengths, encouraging a more positive self-image.

3. Building Resilience: Chapter 12 highlights the significance of resilience in overcoming challenges. It provides strategies for developing resilience in kids, empowering them to bounce back from setbacks and build a stronger sense of self.

4. Promoting Positive Self-Talk: McIntyre introduces the power of positive self-talk and its role in shaping a child's self-esteem. Practical tips are provided to help kids reframe negative thoughts, fostering a more optimistic and empowering mindset.

5. Encouraging a Supportive Environment: The chapter emphasizes the crucial role of a supportive environment in boosting a child's self-esteem. Practical suggestions are given to parents, educators, and peers to create a positive atmosphere that nurtures a child's confidence.

## Reflection Questions

1. How does recognizing and addressing low self-esteem contribute to a child's overall well-being?

-----------------------------------------------------------

-----------------------------------------------------------

-----------------------------------------------------------

-----------------------------------------------------------

-----------------------------------------------------------

-----------------------------------------------------------

2. In what ways can negative labels impact a child's self-perception, and how can you actively work to avoid using such labels?

-----------------------------------------------------------

-----------------------------------------------------------

-----------------------------------------------------------

-----------------------------------------------------------

-----------------------------------------------------------

-----------------------------------------------------------

3. Reflect on instances where resilience played a role in overcoming challenges in your own life or the life of a child you know. What strategies were employed to build resilience?

-----------------------------------------------------------

-----------------------------------------------------------

-----------------------------------------------------------

-----------------------------------------------------------

---------------------------------------------------------------

---------------------------------------------------------------

4. How can positive self-talk be incorporated into daily routines to reinforce a child's positive self-image?

---------------------------------------------------------------

---------------------------------------------------------------

---------------------------------------------------------------

---------------------------------------------------------------

---------------------------------------------------------------

---------------------------------------------------------------

5. In what specific ways can you, as a parent or caregiver, create a supportive environment that fosters a child's confidence and self-esteem?

---------------------------------------------------------------

---------------------------------------------------------------

---------------------------------------------------------------

---------------------------------------------------------------

---------------------------------------------------------------

-----------------------------------------------------------------

6. Think about a time when someone's positive encouragement had a significant impact on your self-esteem. How can you replicate that support for a child in your life?

-----------------------------------------------------------------

-----------------------------------------------------------------

-----------------------------------------------------------------

-----------------------------------------------------------------

-----------------------------------------------------------------

-----------------------------------------------------------------

7. Consider the role of peer relationships in shaping a child's self-esteem. How can you promote positive interactions and discourage negative behaviors among peers?

-----------------------------------------------------------------

-----------------------------------------------------------------

-----------------------------------------------------------------

-----------------------------------------------------------------

---------------------------------------------------------------

---------------------------------------------------------------

8. Reflect on the impact of media and societal expectations on children's self-esteem. How can you mitigate negative influences and reinforce positive messages?

---------------------------------------------------------------

---------------------------------------------------------------

---------------------------------------------------------------

---------------------------------------------------------------

---------------------------------------------------------------

---------------------------------------------------------------

9. Explore activities and hobbies that align with a child's strengths. How can these activities be incorporated into their routine to boost their confidence?

---------------------------------------------------------------

---------------------------------------------------------------

---------------------------------------------------------------

---------------------------------------------------------

---------------------------------------------------------

---------------------------------------------------------

10. Reflect on the language you use when providing feedback to a child. How can you ensure that your words contribute to building their self-esteem rather than undermining it?

---------------------------------------------------------

---------------------------------------------------------

---------------------------------------------------------

---------------------------------------------------------

---------------------------------------------------------

---------------------------------------------------------

## Why am I in a program for Kids with BD?
## How did the school decide that I have BD?
## Key Lessons

1. Understanding the Evaluation Process: In this chapter, the author delves into the process through which schools assess and determine behavioral disorders (BD) in students. The lesson here is to comprehend the comprehensive evaluation procedures that schools follow to make such important decisions.

2. Importance of Collaboration: One key takeaway is the significance of collaboration between parents, teachers, and other school professionals in the evaluation process. Effective communication and cooperation are essential for accurate assessments and ensuring the best possible support for the student.

3. Recognition of Behavioral Patterns: The chapter emphasizes the identification and recognition of consistent behavioral patterns. Understanding these patterns is crucial for both parents and educators to gain insights into a child's behavior and provide targeted interventions.

4. Exploring Alternatives: The author highlights the importance of exploring alternative explanations for a child's behavior. It's crucial to consider various factors that may contribute to behavioral challenges before settling on a diagnosis, reinforcing the idea that a comprehensive approach is necessary.

5. Advocacy for Your Child: A key lesson is the need for parents to advocate for their child throughout the evaluation process. Being actively involved, asking questions, and seeking

clarification ensures that the child's best interests are prioritized.

## Reflection Questions

1. What specific steps can you take to better understand the evaluation process for behavioral disorders in schools?

------------------------------------------------------------

------------------------------------------------------------

------------------------------------------------------------

------------------------------------------------------------

------------------------------------------------------------

------------------------------------------------------------

2. In what ways can you enhance collaboration with your child's teachers and school professionals to contribute to the evaluation process?

------------------------------------------------------------

------------------------------------------------------------

------------------------------------------------------------

------------------------------------------------------------

------------------------------------------------------------

------------------------------------------------------------

3. How might recognizing consistent behavioral patterns assist you in better understanding your child's challenges and needs?

---------------------------------------------------------------

---------------------------------------------------------------

---------------------------------------------------------------

---------------------------------------------------------------

---------------------------------------------------------------

---------------------------------------------------------------

4. Can you identify any alternative explanations for your child's behavior that haven't been explored yet? How can you work with the school to consider these alternatives?

---------------------------------------------------------------

---------------------------------------------------------------

---------------------------------------------------------------

---------------------------------------------------------------

---------------------------------------------------------------

---------------------------------------------------------------

5. Reflect on your role as an advocate for your child. What actions can you take to ensure your child's voice is heard and their needs are met throughout the evaluation process?

_____

_____

_____

_____

_____

_____

6. Considering the information in the chapter, how can you actively engage in open and constructive communication with your child's school regarding the evaluation of behavioral challenges?

_____

_____

_____

_____

_____

7. What resources and support systems can you tap into to gain a deeper understanding of your child's behavior and the evaluation process?

------------------------------------------------

------------------------------------------------

------------------------------------------------

------------------------------------------------

------------------------------------------------

------------------------------------------------

8. How do you envision collaborating with teachers to create a more supportive and understanding learning environment for your child, irrespective of the evaluation outcome?

------------------------------------------------

------------------------------------------------

------------------------------------------------

------------------------------------------------

------------------------------------------------

---------------------------------------------------------------

9. Reflect on any moments where you might have overlooked consistent behavioral patterns in your child. How can you use this insight to improve your understanding and support?

---------------------------------------------------------------

---------------------------------------------------------------

---------------------------------------------------------------

---------------------------------------------------------------

---------------------------------------------------------------

---------------------------------------------------------------

10. Considering the lessons from the chapter, what proactive steps can you take to foster a positive and collaborative relationship with your child's school as they navigate the evaluation process for behavioral challenges?

---------------------------------------------------------------

---------------------------------------------------------------

---------------------------------------------------------------

## What is in my IEP?

## Key Lessons

1. Understanding Your Individualized Education Program (IEP):
   Your IEP is a personalized plan designed to support your unique learning needs. It's crucial to comprehend the components of your IEP and how they contribute to your academic success.
2. Identifying Accommodations and Modifications:
   Dive into the specifics of the accommodations and modifications outlined in your IEP. Recognize how these adjustments are tailored to help you navigate challenges and maximize your learning experience.
3. Advocating for Yourself:
   Your IEP is a tool that empowers you to advocate for your educational needs. Learn how to effectively communicate with teachers, parents, and school staff to ensure that your IEP is implemented to its fullest extent.
4. Setting Personal Goals:
   Take a closer look at the goals outlined in your IEP. These are designed to help you progress

academically and personally. Discover how to set realistic milestones and track your achievements throughout the academic year.

5. Building a Support System:

Your IEP involves collaboration between you, your teachers, and your parents. Understand the importance of this support system and how everyone plays a role in fostering an environment conducive to your success.

## Reflection Questions

1. How does knowing the details of your IEP empower you in the classroom?

-----------------------------------------------------------

-----------------------------------------------------------

-----------------------------------------------------------

-----------------------------------------------------------

-----------------------------------------------------------

-----------------------------------------------------------

2. In what ways do the accommodations and modifications outlined in your IEP contribute to your academic achievements?

-----------------------------------------------------------

-----------------------------------------------------------

------------------------------------------------------------

------------------------------------------------------------

------------------------------------------------------------

------------------------------------------------------------

3. How can you effectively communicate with your teachers and parents about your IEP to ensure a collaborative approach to your education?

------------------------------------------------------------

------------------------------------------------------------

------------------------------------------------------------

------------------------------------------------------------

------------------------------------------------------------

------------------------------------------------------------

4. Reflect on the goals set in your IEP. How do they align with your aspirations, and what steps can you take to achieve them?

------------------------------------------------------------

------------------------------------------------------------

------------------------------------------------------------

-----------------------------------------------------------

-----------------------------------------------------------

-----------------------------------------------------------

5. Considering your IEP, how can you take an active role in advocating for yourself in academic and social settings?

-----------------------------------------------------------

-----------------------------------------------------------

-----------------------------------------------------------

-----------------------------------------------------------

-----------------------------------------------------------

-----------------------------------------------------------

6. Who are the key members of your support system regarding your IEP, and how can you actively involve them in your academic journey?

-----------------------------------------------------------

-----------------------------------------------------------

-----------------------------------------------------------

-----------------------------------------------------------

---------------------------------------------------------------

---------------------------------------------------------------

7. Think about the challenges you face in the classroom. How can your IEP help address these challenges and create a more inclusive learning environment?

---------------------------------------------------------------

---------------------------------------------------------------

---------------------------------------------------------------

---------------------------------------------------------------

---------------------------------------------------------------

---------------------------------------------------------------

8. Reflect on a recent academic accomplishment. How did your IEP contribute to this success, and what lessons can you apply moving forward?

---------------------------------------------------------------

---------------------------------------------------------------

---------------------------------------------------------------

---------------------------------------------------------------

---------------------------------------------------------------

---------------------------------------------------------------

9. Consider any adjustments or revisions needed in your IEP. How can you communicate these needs effectively with the relevant parties?

---------------------------------------------------------------

---------------------------------------------------------------

---------------------------------------------------------------

---------------------------------------------------------------

---------------------------------------------------------------

---------------------------------------------------------------

10. In what ways can you share insights about your IEP with classmates to foster understanding and support within the school community?

---------------------------------------------------------------

---------------------------------------------------------------

---------------------------------------------------------------

---------------------------------------------------------------

---------------------------------------------------------------

---------------------------------------------------------------

# Why aren't I in the regular education class?

## Key Lessons

1. Understanding Individual Needs:
Chapter 13 delves into the importance of recognizing and addressing individual needs. It highlights that being in a different educational setting might be necessary to provide the support and resources required for optimal learning.
2. Embracing Differences:
The chapter emphasizes the significance of embracing differences and understanding that each student has unique strengths and challenges. It encourages you to appreciate diversity within the learning environment.
3. Advocating for Yourself:
A crucial lesson is learning to advocate for yourself and understanding that being in a different educational setting doesn't define your worth. This section empowers you to express your needs and preferences regarding your education.
4. Building a Support Network:
Chapter 13 underscores the importance of building a strong support network. It highlights that being in a specialized class can offer an environment where you can receive specialized assistance, fostering personal and academic growth.

5. Developing Self-Awareness:

The chapter encourages self-reflection and self-awareness. It suggests that by understanding your strengths and challenges, you can actively participate in creating a positive learning experience for yourself.

## Reflection Questions

1. What specific needs do you believe led to the decision for you not to be in the regular education class, and how can those needs be effectively addressed?

------------------------------------------------------------

------------------------------------------------------------

------------------------------------------------------------

------------------------------------------------------------

------------------------------------------------------------

------------------------------------------------------------

2. How have your unique strengths been acknowledged and nurtured in your current educational setting?

------------------------------------------------------------

------------------------------------------------------------

---------------------------------------------------------

---------------------------------------------------------

---------------------------------------------------------

---------------------------------------------------------

3. In what ways have you embraced and celebrated the differences among your peers in the specialized class?

---------------------------------------------------------

---------------------------------------------------------

---------------------------------------------------------

---------------------------------------------------------

---------------------------------------------------------

---------------------------------------------------------

4. Reflect on a time when you advocated for yourself regarding your education. What was the outcome, and how did it contribute to your growth?

---------------------------------------------------------

---------------------------------------------------------

---------------------------------------------------------

---------------------------------------------------------

---------------------------------------------------------

---------------------------------------------------------

5. Who are the key members of your support network within your current educational setting, and how do they positively impact your learning experience?

6. What strategies have you developed to maintain a positive self-image despite being in a specialized class?

---------------------------------------------------------

---------------------------------------------------------

---------------------------------------------------------

---------------------------------------------------------

---------------------------------------------------------

---------------------------------------------------------

7. In what ways have you contributed to creating a supportive and inclusive environment for your peers in the specialized class?

------------------------------------------------------------

------------------------------------------------------------

------------------------------------------------------------

------------------------------------------------------------

------------------------------------------------------------

------------------------------------------------------------

8. How has your understanding of your strengths and challenges evolved since being in the specialized class, and how has this awareness influenced your approach to learning?

------------------------------------------------------------

------------------------------------------------------------

------------------------------------------------------------

------------------------------------------------------------

------------------------------------------------------------

------------------------------------------------------------

9. Reflect on a specific instance where you felt your needs were not adequately addressed in the

regular education class. How does your current educational setting better meet those needs?

------------------------------------------------------------

------------------------------------------------------------

------------------------------------------------------------

------------------------------------------------------------

------------------------------------------------------------

------------------------------------------------------------

10. What steps can you take to actively participate in the decision-making process regarding your educational placement and support services?

------------------------------------------------------------

------------------------------------------------------------

------------------------------------------------------------

------------------------------------------------------------

------------------------------------------------------------

------------------------------------------------------------

## What if I don't want to go back to regular classes?

## Key Lessons

1. Understanding Your Feelings:
Acknowledge and explore your emotions about returning to regular classes. It's essential to recognize and understand your feelings before making decisions about your education.

2. Identifying Concerns and Hurdles:
Take the time to pinpoint specific concerns or challenges that may be contributing to your reluctance to go back to regular classes. Identifying these issues is the first step toward finding viable solutions.

3. Effective Communication:
Learn to express your thoughts and concerns effectively. Whether it's discussing your apprehensions with a teacher, counselor, or parent, effective communication is crucial in finding support and understanding.

4. Exploring Alternatives:
Consider alternative educational options that align with your needs and preferences. There may be alternative programs or learning environments that better suit your learning style and help you thrive academically.

5. Goal Setting and Planning:
Set realistic goals for yourself regarding your education. Establish a plan that incorporates your aspirations and addresses any challenges you may face. Breaking down the process into manageable steps can make the transition more achievable.

## Reflection Questions

1. How would you describe your current emotions and thoughts about returning to regular classes?

--------------------------------------------------------

--------------------------------------------------------

--------------------------------------------------------

--------------------------------------------------------

--------------------------------------------------------

--------------------------------------------------------

2. What specific challenges or concerns do you associate with going back to regular classes, and how might you address them?

--------------------------------------------------------

--------------------------------------------------------

--------------------------------------------------------

--------------------------------------------------------

--------------------------------------------------------

--------------------------------------------------------

3. In what ways can effective communication with

teachers, parents, or counselors positively impact your decision-making process?

------------------------------------------------------------

------------------------------------------------------------

------------------------------------------------------------

------------------------------------------------------------

------------------------------------------------------------

------------------------------------------------------------

4. Have you explored alternative educational options that might better suit your learning preferences? If not, what steps can you take to investigate these alternatives?

------------------------------------------------------------

------------------------------------------------------------

------------------------------------------------------------

------------------------------------------------------------

------------------------------------------------------------

------------------------------------------------------------

5. What short-term and long-term goals do you

have for your education, and how can you break them down into achievable steps?

-----------------------------------------------------------

-----------------------------------------------------------

-----------------------------------------------------------

-----------------------------------------------------------

-----------------------------------------------------------

-----------------------------------------------------------

6. Who can you turn to for support and guidance as you navigate your feelings and decisions about returning to regular classes?

-----------------------------------------------------------

-----------------------------------------------------------

-----------------------------------------------------------

-----------------------------------------------------------

-----------------------------------------------------------

-----------------------------------------------------------

7. What steps can you take to improve your

communication skills, ensuring that your thoughts and concerns are effectively conveyed to others?

----------------------------------------------------------

----------------------------------------------------------

----------------------------------------------------------

----------------------------------------------------------

----------------------------------------------------------

----------------------------------------------------------

8. How do you envision your ideal learning environment, and are there aspects of regular classes that align with or deviate from this vision?

----------------------------------------------------------

----------------------------------------------------------

----------------------------------------------------------

----------------------------------------------------------

----------------------------------------------------------

----------------------------------------------------------

9. What are the potential benefits and drawbacks of exploring alternative educational options, and

how can you weigh these factors in your decision-making process?

------------------------------------------------------------

------------------------------------------------------------

------------------------------------------------------------

------------------------------------------------------------

------------------------------------------------------------

------------------------------------------------------------

10. Considering your aspirations and preferences, what adjustments can you make to your educational plan to ensure a successful and fulfilling academic journey?

------------------------------------------------------------

------------------------------------------------------------

------------------------------------------------------------

------------------------------------------------------------

------------------------------------------------------------

------------------------------------------------------------

# Final self-assessment queries

1. Reflecting on Achievements:
   - What accomplishments are you most proud of during this period of assessment?
   - How have your achievements aligned with your initial goals and expectations?

---------------------------------------------------------------

---------------------------------------------------------------

---------------------------------------------------------------

---------------------------------------------------------------

---------------------------------------------------------------

---------------------------------------------------------------

2. Personal Growth and Development:

   - In what ways have you personally grown or developed throughout this period?
   - Are there specific skills or qualities you feel you have enhanced, and how have they contributed to your overall growth?

---------------------------------------------------------------

---------------------------------------------------------------

---------------------------------------------------------------

---------------------------------------------------------------

-------------------------------------------------------------
-------------------------------------------------------------

3. Challenges and Overcoming Obstacles:

- What challenges did you encounter, and how did you navigate through them?
- Can you identify specific strategies or coping mechanisms that helped you overcome obstacles?

-------------------------------------------------------------
-------------------------------------------------------------
-------------------------------------------------------------
-------------------------------------------------------------
-------------------------------------------------------------

4. Learning and Knowledge Acquisition:

- What new knowledge or insights have you gained during this timeframe?
- How have you applied your learning to real-life situations or challenges?

-------------------------------------------------------------
-------------------------------------------------------------
-------------------------------------------------------------
-------------------------------------------------------------

-------------------------------------------------------------

-------------------------------------------------------------

## 5. Collaboration and Communication:

- How effectively have you collaborated with others in your personal or professional life?
- Have there been instances where communication played a crucial role in achieving positive outcomes?

-------------------------------------------------------------

-------------------------------------------------------------

-------------------------------------------------------------

-------------------------------------------------------------

-------------------------------------------------------------

-------------------------------------------------------------

## 6. Time Management and Productivity:

- Reflect on your time management skills. How have you prioritized tasks and managed your time efficiently?
- Are there areas where you could improve in terms of productivity and time utilization?

-------------------------------------------------------------

-------------------------------------------------------------

-----------------------------------------------------------

-----------------------------------------------------------

-----------------------------------------------------------

-----------------------------------------------------------

## 7. Adaptability and Flexibility:

- Describe situations where you demonstrated adaptability and flexibility.
- How have you embraced change, and what have you learned from adapting to new circumstances?

-----------------------------------------------------------

-----------------------------------------------------------

-----------------------------------------------------------

-----------------------------------------------------------

-----------------------------------------------------------

-----------------------------------------------------------

## 8. Setting and Reassessing Goals:

- Evaluate the goals you set for yourself. Which ones were achieved, and which ones were not?
- How have your goals evolved throughout the assessment period, and have any adjustments been necessary?

----------------------------------------------------------

----------------------------------------------------------

----------------------------------------------------------

----------------------------------------------------------

----------------------------------------------------------

----------------------------------------------------------

## 9. Feedback and Continuous Improvement:

- How have you sought and incorporated feedback from others into your personal and professional development?
- What specific actions have you taken to continuously improve your skills and performance?

----------------------------------------------------------

----------------------------------------------------------

----------------------------------------------------------

----------------------------------------------------------

----------------------------------------------------------

----------------------------------------------------------

## 10. Work-Life Balance:

- Assess your work-life balance during this period. How well have you managed the demands of your personal and professional life?

- Are there areas where you need to make adjustments to achieve a healthier balance?

------------------------------------------------------------

------------------------------------------------------------

------------------------------------------------------------

------------------------------------------------------------

------------------------------------------------------------

------------------------------------------------------------

11. Impact on Others:

- Reflect on the impact you have had on those around you—both personally and professionally.
- How have your actions positively influenced others, and are there areas where you could enhance your positive impact?

------------------------------------------------------------

------------------------------------------------------------

------------------------------------------------------------

------------------------------------------------------------

------------------------------------------------------------

------------------------------------------------------------

12. Future Planning:

- Consider your future aspirations and goals. How do you plan to build upon your current successes and address areas for improvement?

- What steps will you take to ensure continued personal and professional growth in the upcoming period?

---------------------------------------------------------------

---------------------------------------------------------------

---------------------------------------------------------------

---------------------------------------------------------------

---------------------------------------------------------------

---------------------------------------------------------------

---------------------------------------------------------------

Made in the USA
Coppell, TX
02 November 2024

39520306R00193